W9-CDN-202

Training and Collaboration with

Virtual Worlds

Training and Collaboration with
Virtual Worlds

How to Create Cost-Saving, Efficient, and Engaging Programs

ALEX HEIPHETZ, PH.D., AND GARY WOODILL, ED.D.

New York Chicago San Francisco Lisbon London Madrid Mexico City
Milan New Delhi San Juan Seoul Singapore Sydney Toronto

The *McGraw·Hill* Companies

1 2 3 4 5 6 7 8 9 10 11 12 13 14 15 16 17 18 19 20 21 22   DOC/DOC   0 9

ISBN 978-0-07-162802-0
MHID   0-07-162802-9

Interior design by Susan H. Hartman

McGraw-Hill books are available at special quantity discounts to use as premiums and sales promotions or for use in corporate training programs. To contact a representative, please e-mail us at bulksales@mcgraw-hill.com.

Contents

Contents

Preface

as Second Life rapidly matures, technological quirks that used to keep corporate users at arm's length fade away. In their place, companies can find powerful business applications, particularly in the training, collaboration, technical support, human resources, and marketing fields. Minimizing travel, efficiently managing geographically dispersed teams, and training new generations of workers that are coming into the workplace to replace baby boomers are no longer support functions but matters of survival. Case studies on the use of virtual worlds from business leaders around the world suggest that virtual worlds are a tool that must become an intrinsic part of any comprehensive business-development effort.

Previous books on Second Life and other virtual worlds have concentrated on entertainment value and use by hobbyists. In this first book on corporate use of virtual worlds, we make an experience-based case for, and describe best practices of, Second Life and other virtual worlds as an effective tool for business survival and growth.

Nothing is more valuable in business than experience. We were extremely lucky to receive unprecedented access to virtual world pioneers from the corporate community. Contributors from many well-known

American and international organizations candidly shared both the successes they had and the problems they faced, as well as best practices and recommendations drawn from their experience and experimentation with the virtual worlds.

In this book we discuss everything you need to learn about the business uses of virtual worlds, with an emphasis on Second Life: what it is, what you need to start a successful program in Second Life or other virtual worlds, what to expect, and how these innovative environments are used by a variety of well-respected corporate players. We also pay special attention to security issues and concerns, as well as real-life implementations and use of simulations to achieve competitive advantage and a high return on investment (ROI). We hope that you find the book both enjoyable and useful.

Acknowledgments

as authors, we find ourselves in a somewhat awkward position: while, in a few pages, we will talk about necessity of and the best ways to teach teamwork skills, we are extremely lucky to have the opportunity to work with people who did not need any lessons and could serve as a model of a fantastic team. This book was conceived as a practical guide. Therefore, we simply *had* to draw on a large network of practitioners and thinkers to have any chance of fulfilling our goal. The following pioneers in the business use of virtual worlds shared their firsthand experience (in the order the case studies appear in the book):

Paul F. Steinberg, Course Architect, Intel
Zain Naboulsi, MSDN Developer Evangelist, Microsoft
Philippe Barreaud, Chief Enterprise Architect, Michelin Group
David M. Antonacci, Director of Teaching & Learning Technologies, University of Kansas Medical Center
Stephanie P. Gerald, Educational Technology Liaison to the School of Allied Health of University of Kansas Medical Center

Russell Miyaki, Vice President, National Interactive Creative Director, TMP Worldwide

Polly Pearson, Vice President, Employment Brand and Strategy Engagement, EMC Corporation

Christopher Bishop, Senior Communication Specialist, Corporate Citizenship and Corporate Affairs, IBM

Dannette Veale, New Media Program Manager, Cisco

Ramin Aliyev, Business Analyst, World Bank

Dahlia Khalifa, Senior Strategy Adviser, World Bank

Ryan Hahn, Consultant, World Bank

Rebecca Ong, Communications Manager, World Bank

We are indebted to professors Anne P. Massey of Indiana University and Mitzi Montoya of North Carolina State University and doctoral candidate Valerie Bartelt of Indiana University, who kindly shared with us methodology and results of their research of Second Life prior to an official publication.

Mark Kingdon, CEO of Linden Lab, provided a unique glimpse inside the company behind Second Life and its approach to working with corporate users. Of course, without Linden Lab and Second Life, the business use of virtual worlds would have remained a narrow-niche business, never attracting the attention of corporate users.

A round of applause goes to Emily Carleton, editor at McGraw-Hill Professional, who came up with the idea of the book and had the tenacity and nerve to bet on somebody who is more used to doing the things described in this book than writing about them. As a reward, she had to do heavy-lifting editing of the text.

From Alex Heiphetz

Thanks to my wife, Sveta, and son, Mark, who, for many months, got to hear me growling, "I've got to work on the book; I don't have time," rather than the usual, "Let's go sailing/skiing/something." I don't know where they got the patience to live with me in the first place! Thanks to my extended family and close friends who made me what I am today. Finally, very special thanks goes to all the nonbelievers, to those who failed at Second Life, and, above all, to those who, instead of persevering, were writing never-ending blogs about virtual worlds and Second Life being useless in the corporate world. Your failures taught me more than my successes, and your constant venting served as a source of endless entertainment. Had you been more persistent, your name would be on the cover, not mine.

From Gary Woodill

First, thanks to Alex Heiphetz for asking me to be part of this exciting project. As director of research and analysis at Brandon Hall Research, I am constantly scanning for new learning technologies, presenting webinars and workshops on the latest trends, and posting to Twitter, Facebook, and several blogs. To be able to focus my energies on one area in depth was a refreshing change and a great learning experience. It helps greatly to have such supportive colleagues at Brandon Hall Research, who encouraged me in this work. To Brandon Hall, Richard Nantel, Janet Clarey, Tom Werner, Karen Balcomb, and our hardworking support staff, thanks for making my job enjoyable. Tom Werner, who blogs about virtual worlds with a lot of passion, was especially helpful in supplying us with leads of interesting projects to pursue. Thanks to my wife, Karen Anderson, who, after twenty-five years of marriage, continues to keep me engaged in the real world with her daily support and caring.

Introduction

One of the worst things that can happen to a new technology or a software platform is to receive a lukewarm reception. Virtual worlds, especially Second Life, escaped this fate even before they were on the corporate radar. Started in 2000 as a game environment, the virtual world of Second Life caused immediate battles on blogs between its early proponents and adopters, and adherents of the older and more established massively multiplayer online role-playing games (MMORPGs), such as *World of Warcraft*.

The principal difference—and a point of contention for many—between virtual worlds such as Second Life and MMORPGs is the absence of predetermined themes, sets of goals, or preset scenarios in Second Life. But, this is the very element that makes Second Life useful in corporate environments. Traditional MMORPGs are based on established themes such as medieval fantasies with dungeons and dragons, knights and princesses, and swords and sorcery; or science-fiction narratives with time machines and interstellar travel; or other recognizable literary genres. From the outset, multiplayer games have provided participants with the base elements of a scenario that the players develop into a live story, using appropriate tools and sub-scenarios such as fighting battles, slaying monsters, or locating treasure.

Second Life and other similar virtual worlds do not provide such themes or scenarios. When you open an account as a new user, you are free to visit one of the hundreds of thousands, if not millions, of locations. The owners of each place in a virtual world built their particular location to serve their own interests. While you are almost guaranteed to find something of interest, there is no predetermined structure. There are no scenarios to follow, and there are few rules.

Not everybody appreciates that. One of the earliest and most persistent complaints about Second Life from mainstream users, especially those with experience in structured MMORPGs, was precisely the lack of structure, absence of scenarios, and, as a result, "boredom." On the other hand, having an "open sandbox" where *you* establish the rules provides an unlimited opportunity to build your own scenarios and use them for whatever purpose you choose, be it a "knights and dragon quest," a "corporate sales mission," or "enterprise architecture training." Unwittingly, virtual worlds separate those who need a structured environment to be imposed on them from the more creative types who see unlimited opportunity in creating content for themselves, their Second Life communities, and/or their company.

Opinions became sharper and blog wars intensified with the first attempts to use Second Life in a corporate world. While some noncorporate early adopters were busy fending off business-connected newcomers, trying to protect what they saw as their personal turf and their very own freewheeling culture, corporate neophytes were researching capabilities of the new platform and its potential for use in business. Some of the original corporate entrants tried using virtual worlds to market their wares to the gamers. Others were fascinated with the apparent ease of creating a three-dimensional environment and rushed to build exact copies of their corporate campuses. Yet others tried to use the virtual world environment to build and sell their widgets.

Many of the original corporate experiments failed. Some of the early corporate entrants backed out of using virtual worlds. Others, however, in true Darwinian fashion, abandoned failed projects while persevering with and expanding those that seemed to work. By doing this, these pioneering corporate users established the basic parameters of what works and what does not, even though the area is still highly experimental and new developments take place almost every day.

Intended Audience

One of the major challenges in writing this book was to keep it interesting and concise for the extremely diverse audience that is generally involved in designing and implementing virtual world projects in corporate environments. Technical details important to a network security specialist are foreign to an instructional designer. Using virtual worlds as a collaborative tool for geographically dispersed teams would be of interest to operations or engineering professionals, while training simulations and robotic avatars might interest directors of human resources. Stepped implementation procedures and the ROI of these projects are probably closer to the areas of responsibility of C-level executives.

We faced this challenge by using three tactics. First, we identify methodologies that are fundamental to virtual world technology and therefore have to be well understood by everybody involved in a virtual world project. Second, we discuss examples of real-life uses of virtual worlds, with the emphasis on methodology and its implications, focusing on how using virtual worlds can alleviate major problems. Finally, we summarize our findings at the end of each chapter as a series of conclusions and best practices.

The results offer something for every department and member of a typical organization. In addition to developing practical approaches for designing virtual training, collaboration, support, and marketing programs, we also cover in detail advanced topics such as dealing with issues of security, managing asynchronous simulations, and using robotic avatars.

▶ **Instructional designers** can take advantage of the practical approaches to creating many types of training described in this book and can use concrete information on establishing training programs in virtual worlds. Experience-based instructional design approaches, examples of already existing and effective virtual world–based training, and descriptions of existing tools for creating content in Second Life are all covered.

▶ **Human resources professionals** will be interested in information on using virtual worlds for recruiting, new-hire orientation, and soft-skills training.

▶ **Directors of training and training managers** will find valuable data on the areas of training that gain most from expanding into virtual worlds. They will see how a virtual world platform can help fill the gaps in existing training programs, resulting in better outcomes and increased ROI. They will also learn how to design new types of efficient training programs, blend new virtual world training into existing distance learning programs, and connect virtual world programs with learning management systems (LMS) and databases.

▶ **Department heads** will be interested in data on managing geographically dispersed teams, improving team collaboration, and implementing leadership training.

▶ **Marketing professionals** will find it informative to read about one of the first successful marketing campaigns in Second Life and learn what made this campaign successful. After significant failed attempts to market in virtual worlds, it appears we are finally making serious progress in using the platform for successful marketing projects.

▶ **Directors and C-level executives** can take advantage of the concise review of a number of Fortune 100 company projects in Second Life and other virtual worlds and the information on the current state of affairs in this area.

Organization of the Book

Each chapter of this book takes you into a rich set of topics, many of which could be expanded into separate books on their own. However, we move quickly to discuss all the topics and data you need to know for a solid introduction to this field. Extensive references in each chapter point to more resources for further exploration.

Chapter 1, "Virtual Worlds: What's in It for the Corporate World?," weaves together many threads of discussion: What are virtual worlds? Why do you want your company to use them and what for? How do people behave in virtual worlds as compared to the real world? What are the benefits of real-time global communications? How do we ensure that a virtual world is both employee- and company-friendly?

Chapter 2, "Enterprise Applications of Virtual Worlds," gives an overview of virtual world business-use cases.

Chapter 3, "Virtual Worlds: Selecting the Best," offers our outlook on existing virtual world platforms. Based on experience, we provide criteria for selecting the platform that is right for you out of many available virtual worlds. After a brief description of existing virtual worlds, we concentrate on five that are best suited for enterprise use.

Chapter 4, "Linden Lab and Second Life in Their Own Words: Enterprise-Related Developments and Future Plans," is based on an interview with Mark Kingdon, CEO of Linden Lab, the company that created Second Life. We discuss the most important topics that often cause concern in the corporate world: network security, ability to place Second Life on your own network behind the firewall, and platform stability.

Chapter 5, "Deploying a Corporate Training Program in Second Life," takes you through the process of establishing your company's Second Life program step-by-step. We start with defining the goals of your project and discussing what works and what does not in the new medium. In the second part of the chapter, we delve into practical matters: What is a Second Life island? Do you want to buy or rent? We discuss building an environment, instructional design considerations, and security, as well as tools that help you to create content.

Chapter 6, "First Steps in a Virtual World: Synchronous Training and Lectures," describes presentations and instructions in a virtual world. This appears to be one of the standard entry points into virtual worlds for many early adopters. Zain Naboulsi, Microsoft MSDN developer evangelist, and Paul Steinberg, course architect at Intel, share their experiences in creating similar projects. Both companies used Second Life to successfully build a community of developers, emphasizing growing horizontal links among developers, self-help, exchange of ideas, technical support, and new-product launches.

In Chapter 7, "Teaching Complex Concepts in a New Way: The Michelin Group Case Study," Philippe Barreaud, chief enterprise architect at Michelin, provides a unique case study. The Michelin Group is known as a highly innovative company, but its Second Life project was not a case of innovation for its own sake. Michelin staff felt they had to start their Second Life training program simply because all the standard approaches they tried before had failed miserably. The case study provides a detailed description of the methodology the company used that resulted in success, when none of the traditional approaches made the grade.

Chapter 8, "Teamwork and Leadership in Virtual Worlds," describes methods and simulations used in virtual worlds for teamwork and leadership training, as well as the theoretical foundations that make it possible to (a) successfully teach qualities that at one time were considered innate and (b) do so in virtual worlds.

Chapter 9, "Doing It Asynchronously: Training Simulations in Second Life," defines training simulations and distinguishes among person-to-object, person-to-person, and person-to-robot simulations. We are still far away from using artificial intelligence with virtual worlds, but the opportunity to use robotic avatars as a part of your communication training, new-hire orientation, or other projects is a significant advantage of Second Life.

In Chapter 10, "Procedural Training in Second Life: University of Kansas Medical Center Case Study," David M. Antonacci, director of teaching and learning technologies, and Stephanie P. Gerald, educational technology liaison to the School of Allied Health of the University of Kansas Medical Center, share information about their Second Life nurse-training project. Preparing a patient for a surgery is a complex medical procedure. Teaching it in Second Life is a great example of procedural training, which involves multiple steps with numerous decision points. Second Life provides trainees with a safe and controlled learning space that is well suited for this type of training.

Chapter 11, "Recruiting and New-Hire Orientation: TMP Worldwide, EMC Corporation, and IBM Case Studies," provides some background on recruiting and new-hire orientation, and then immediately proceeds to the case studies written by Russell Miyaki, vice president and national interactive creative director of TMP Worldwide; Polly Pearson, vice president of employment brand and strategy engagement of EMC Corporation; and Christopher Bishop, senior communication specialist of corporate citizenship and corporate affairs at IBM. Together, these case studies present best practices for using Second Life in human resources projects. They also demonstrate that Second Life became common enough to be used as a cost-effective tool in recruiting and new-hire orientation, and that virtual world events attract the right type of candidates for both technology and nontechnology companies.

Chapter 12, "Enterprise Collaboration: The Virtual World Application," depicts several working approaches to collaboration. Dannette Veale, new media program manager at Cisco, describes how her company took advantage of the Second Life environment as an opportunity to communicate and collaborate with customers and partners. On the other end of the spectrum is the Second Life project of the World Bank. Ramin Aliyev, a business analyst in the World Bank Group's Financial and Private Sector Development Vice Presidency; Dahlia Khalifa, senior strategy adviser of the World Bank Group's Doing Business project; Ryan Hahn, a consultant for the World Bank Group's Financial and Private Sector Development Vice Presidency; and Rebecca Ong, communications manager at World Bank, take an unconventional look at marketing as a collaborative activity. The result is perhaps the most successful Second Life marketing campaign to date.

Finally, Chapter 13, "The Future of Employee Training in Virtual Worlds," summarizes our findings and provides an outlook of virtual world development in the corporate world in a close- to midrange time perspective.

Chapters 1, 3–6, the first half of chapter 8, and chapters 9–12 were written by Dr. Alex Heiphetz with use of original project data provided and interviews given by respective sources. Chapters 2, 13, and the second half of chapter 8 were written by Dr. Gary Woodill. Chapter 7 was written by Philippe Barreaud and Dr. Alex Heiphetz. The two main authors actively commented on and edited each other's and the other contributor's materials but, surprisingly, managed to remain friends nevertheless.

The references list a number of books, research papers, news articles, blogs, and conference presentations that we used in our work. The authors also created a website, www.TheVirtualWorldBook.com, so that readers can access the latest information on using virtual worlds in corporate environments and contact us.

Virtual Worlds: What's in It for the Corporate World?

You probably have plenty of technologies already at work in your organization. Do you even need to consider what virtual worlds (VWs, as we'll occasionally refer to them in this book) can offer you? In size and expenditures, your IT department already rivals a small kingdom, and your staff is always ask-

> *"A perfection of means, and confusion of aims, seems to be our main problem."*
> —*Albert Einstein*

ing for more. Why bother with a new, "unproven" technology? You have seen more than one promising tool turn out to be a total fiasco.

Perhaps you've heard that virtual worlds can cut costs. Well, we'll be honest with you: *virtual worlds do not provide cost savings*. You read it right—no cost savings. What they *do* provide is *cost avoidance*. That's how they increase productivity and add to your bottom line—by eliminating opportunities to spend money. If this is not the result you are looking for, do not waste your time reading this book. If it is of interest, let's see how we can avoid traditional costs without damaging existing, time-tested processes and, in many cases, improving them.

The mere availability of a technology does not mean that you will benefit from it; nor does it mean that those in a position to benefit will know how and when to use it. The good news is that, conceptually, virtual worlds are easy to understand, and integrating them into a corporate setting is in many ways similar to assimilating the Internet in the mid- to late 1990s. Corporate communications, information systems, training, marketing, customer support—all of these changed drastically during that time. The same change management methods that worked then are useful when deploying virtual worlds today.

Dealing with business transformation often makes you wish you had an extra pair of eyes and ears, as so much attention is required across the enterprise. We cannot recommend a method of growing extra eyes, but having an efficient training program that fully encompasses the entire production cycle will help almost as well. Besides fulfilling the need to train anybody and everybody, training deals with all levels of personnel, all kinds of human interactions, and all facets of technology. Therefore, in addition to its direct utility, it is a convenient, forward-looking indicator of the impact of any changes in an organization, including adoption and acceptance of new technology. Given the recent shift toward always-accessible e-learning, student self-reliance, immersive learning, and simulations, using training as a sensor of change is all the more attractive.

 ## The Use of Simulations

Simulations have proved their worth since they became a cornerstone of training in areas as diverse as the space program and medicine. In this context, "simulations" mean expensive and expansive machinery and software that replicates "the real thing" by using complex technology to create a full impression of the reality of a process in a trainee's mind. Passenger jet simulators, for example, use computer-generated, three-dimensional images reproducing views out of the flight deck windows. The hydraulic legs of these machines are capable of moving the simulator in all directions, and even briefly accelerating and decelerating. The expense of building and using complex simulators—full-flight simulators cost up to $20 million to buy and $800 an hour to "fly" (Boeing 1995)— precludes significant growth of their use outside of the life-critical applications in a few industries.

Fortunately, the past ten years have seen development of simulations that require only a computer and, perhaps, a high-speed network connection. They started out as little more than a series of slides introducing a trainee to an educational situation. The trainee had to find a solution by selecting answers from a menu. Within a few years of their introduction, these simulations acquired the ability to use and reuse video and audio fragments, PowerPoint slides, spreadsheets, and other documents.

As anybody who has ever faced doing several presentations over a short time will agree, recycling old slides can be a great idea, so it is easy to understand the appeal of using such simulations and the tools for creating them. The problem, however, is that these are not *really* simulations in the sense that flight simulators are. Within the training context, simulation is a technique *imitating* experience in a real situation, interaction, or process via an artificially created guided experience. The experience does not have to replicate reality in the way a flight simulator replicates the flight deck experience. It must, however, have sufficient *cognitive realism* to work (Smith 1986; Herrington et al. 2007). That is, simulations must interactively evoke principal aspects of the real world, enabling and motivating students to learn.

A simulation does not simply tell learners what and how to do something; rather, it encourages thinking, acting, testing different approaches, and pursuing different strategies. Learners respond to the environment, questions, and other stimuli so that they can discover solutions on their own after having worked through several iterations. This is something best done with an *immersive simulation*—that is, a simulation presenting realistic models of an environment. Good immersive simulations allow for more than one path to success. Generally, they require (and, therefore, teach) flexibility as opposed to rigid, prescriptive behaviors that characterize other types of learning.

There's a whole alphabet of learning tools, from *Adobe Captivate* to *Wink*. But virtual worlds are the only type of platform that allows you to create truly immersive situations *and* the only one where already existing tools—some of them free—allow nontechnical personnel to create highly technical simulations, again helping you *avoid* the costs of using competing technologies. Virtual worlds are in no way limited to training: they can be used for collaborative and brainstorming meetings, conferences, human resources management, sales, technical support, and marketing, to name a few.

Participants represented by graphical avatars communicate and work together with others' avatars and robotic avatars (run by sophisticated computer programs) to operate models of equipment or programmable training tools. Unlike simulations created specifically to teach one subject, or even one facet of a complex issue, virtual worlds work as a "device driver," providing multiple participants simultaneous access to a computer-created environment. (Side note: A device driver is a computer program that allows higher-level programs, such as spreadsheet or word processing programs, to interact with a piece of hardware, such as a printer or a flash drive. High-level programs do not need to know how to communicate with each particular brand of hardware. It is the device driver's business to take commands from a high-level program and translate them into something the hardware can understand.)

Human Behavior in a Virtual World

Compared with other tools, virtual worlds from the outset provide much greater capability in creating immersive environments. However, prior to re-creating anything related to the physical world (PhW) in a virtual world we have to ask an important question: do we, as humans, behave in VW in the same way that we would in our physical world? If the answer is no, then we may as well rephrase the old saying about Las Vegas, "What happens in a virtual world, stays in a virtual world," rather than depending on virtual worlds for learning anything serious.

Luckily, the answer is yes. As shown by the pioneering work of Professors Mitzi Montoya of the business management department at North Carolina State University and Anne Massey of the Kelley School of Business at Indiana University, in Second Life, people do feel and behave very similarly in virtual and physical worlds (Montoya and Massey 2008). We can be confident that high-level immersive environments, such as Second Life, can be used for training and other corporate functions and the results achieved there can be extrapolated into the physical world.

 ## Virtual Collaboration

The most obvious feature any newcomer notices when introduced to virtual worlds is the ability to communicate remotely. Indeed, you do not need special training to use virtual worlds as a communication tool in order to quickly build rapport with your colleagues around the globe. As noted by Christopher Bishop of IBM, "Virtual worlds make geography history."

Communication in all its aspects is the point of entry into virtual worlds for many organizations, especially since it can be tied into both existing communication venues and new social media projects. People work together, talk, and establish informal support networks as if they were working in the same room, but without the need to travel—an important consideration when budgets are as tight as time.

There are plenty of examples of collaboration projects that use virtual worlds—and several successful ones, such as EMC Corporation's recruiting effort, Microsoft's IT Pros developer groups, and Cisco Systems' use of

Second Life as a customer relations management tool, are profiled later in this book. However, virtual worlds would not have generated such intense discussion over the past several years and most certainly would not have deserved this book if they were used merely as a communications tool—there are many more areas of corporate use.

 ## Corporate Training in Virtual Worlds

Any human activity, no matter how interesting and enticing, has aspects that can be boring. Some of them can be compared to memorizing the telephone directory, except that most of the time the subject matter is harder to visualize and understand. Virtual worlds have proved to be a great tool for training personnel in this situation. For example, Crompco used Second Life to archive information about underground storage tanks and train employees on the physical aspects of a service station (Business-Week 2006). This training allowed employees to better understand their working environment, promoting more knowledgeable and safer behavior on the job.

In general, Second Life seems to be a uniquely appropriate platform for all kinds of procedural and 3-D visualization training—the kind of training where other available methods require a significantly longer time and a more sizable investment. Take, for example, the complex and highly technical subject of enterprise architecture. In a greatly simplified form, enterprise architecture can be defined as a conceptual skeleton determining how an organization can most effectively achieve its current and future objectives within an efficient information technology environment. Even this simplified definition might make you cringe.

Michael Platt of Microsoft (Platt 2009) describes enterprise architecture as containing four points of view: the business perspective (processes and standards of day-to-day operations), the application perspective (interactions among the processes and standards), the information perspective (data that an organization needs to operate, such as documents and databases), and the technology perspective (hardware, operating systems, programming, and networking solutions). Teaching and learning such a complicated subject, which encompasses all facets of corporate operations, is not easy, especially because it requires a lot of memorizing of information as exciting as a phone directory. One of the reasons Michelin pioneered teaching enterprise architecture in Second Life, as you will read about later in the book, was the inadequacy of alternative methods. As a result, they significantly improved the outcome of training, as well as learners' perceptions of the subject and its importance.

Using Virtual Worlds for Marketing and Branding

Although marketing and branding can be viewed as a part of communication activities, they deserve a separate discussion. Early attempts at using virtual worlds for marketing, based on leading approaches on the Web or in the physical world, led to a series of high-profile spectacular flops. As a result, a brief period of intensive activity in the Second Life marketing sector came to a screeching halt as "bleeding edge" pioneers curtailed their efforts and others chose to sit on the fence.

The fundamentals of Second Life, however, turned out to be enticing enough for a few brave companies to continue working in the area on shoestring budgets. Second Life, as the most populated consumer-oriented virtual world, allows you to quickly and, yes, affordably connect with consumers in places where they spend lots of time, creating brand awareness and building loyalty. You can do that by providing inexpensive but appealing virtual experiences (contests, auto-paying jobs, freebies, live in-world events, etc.) for your target audience. More important, you can begin a conversation with potential customers, learning how to best leverage your virtual world presence for future sales. In the process, you will reinforce your reputation as a forward-thinking, successful company and start to build a community of loyal customers. The World Bank example (see the case study in Chapter 12) shows that Second Life is a great tool for reaching a wide audience in a short period of time while getting extensive media coverage. TMP Worldwide Advertising & Communications blended recruiting and marketing efforts by using Second Life for targeted recruitment projects, while enhancing branding for such clients as GE, Accenture, and US Cellular (see the case study in Chapter 11). In other words, rumors of Second Life's marketing death turned out to be an exaggeration. The lesson to be learned is that simply projecting your marketing experiences from other media into Second Life, rather than designing a new medium-specific strategy, will probably lead to failure.

Making Virtual Worlds Employee-Friendly

A word of caution (and managing expectations) is in order: you will be well served to make sure that the target audience within your organization will not require excessive special training in order to be able to use virtual worlds. We have encountered horror stories of employees unable to use virtual worlds, and these stories are often quoted to support a case against this technology. However, these are very much the exception rather than the rule.

There are well-documented cases of Second Life being used by retirees and other less computer-literate groups. What, then, is the secret to making sure your target audience uses virtual worlds productively, thereby realizing a good return on investment (ROI) from this new technology? Because a virtual world serves as a layer of abstraction between a user and other users or applications, a user does not need to know how a virtual world or simulation inside a virtual world works. In well-designed cases of corporate use, you can log into a virtual world and start working immediately, using only the most basic, generic computer skills that most of us have.

Facilities to make this possible are generally provided by support services such as instructional designers, marketers, and human resources personnel. Business-friendly virtual worlds provide enough tools to create environments and tasks that clearly relate to real-life situations, without employees having to deal with a steep learning curve unrelated to their training goals. Some virtual worlds, such as Second Life, offer a plethora of built-in and third-party tools. These tools make creating environments and simulations a relatively trouble-free and technically straightforward chore performed via a graphical user interface (GUI). Eliminating a steep learning curve is largely a question of selecting the correct virtual world and the correct tools for the task.

 ## Implementing Virtual World Projects

How hard will it be to implement your specific virtual world project? This is difficult to answer without knowing your specific requirements. But it will take fewer resources than developing custom simulations from scratch, which can run into hundreds of thousands, if not millions, of dollars, depending on the scope of the project.

Astute developers can create environments and tools as they need them. For example, Microsoft spends as little as $2,340 per year to cover the fees for its Second Life developer community projects. Michelin and Intel, on the other hand, spent approximately sixty thousand euros and slightly less than a hundred thousand U.S. dollars, respectively (which, at the then-applicable exchange rate, worked out to approximately the same amount), to develop comprehensive training facilities in Second Life. Was there a substantial difference in the results? As the case studies in subsequent chapters demonstrate, all three companies are quite satisfied with the tangible and intangible results they were able to achieve, and they continue to use their virtual environments.

In general, for an average deployment, the virtual world cost per user is less than the cost of most other training technologies and allows a training department to avoid major costs when used as a replacement for physical world events and communications tools.

We have already noted the similarities between virtual worlds and Web projects. It is also important to underline a major difference between early Web projects and successful virtual world projects, regardless of their respective budgets or original purposes. The difference is that simply "establishing a presence" in this highly interactive environment does not work. All successful projects must set up specific goals, clearly define expectations, and work on receiving formal and informal feedback. Interactivity can be a double-edged sword. It works extremely well when you need to hold a live meeting, training session, or live marketing event. It can also create disappointment when a prospect visits your virtual island and finds nothing but empty buildings.

Enterprise Applications of Virtual Worlds

> "People like to die by the latest method."
> —*Bertrand Russell*

there are many pathways to learning. One way to learn is to read about something and let the words evoke images and concepts in our mind. Words work to stimulate our imagination because they are often metaphors of our physical experiences or because they are descriptions that we can relate to from our own lives.

A more immediate way to learn, however, is from direct experience. Our senses take in information, and our brain processes and integrates this information into our memory, along with all our other experiences. Virtual environments and simulations allow us to get away from learning from words and experience an approximation of the world about which we want to learn. The more realistic the virtual world or simulation, the more we learn from direct experience as opposed to our imagination. Both approaches to learning are valid and have a role in training. Ideally, each approach reinforces the other.

Experiential Learning

How does experiential learning work? Generally there are five phases that the learner goes through in an experiential learning situation. These are (1) experiencing by taking in data with one's senses, (2) sharing and/or reflecting about the experience in order to make sense of it, (3) generalizing in order to develop abstractions and hypotheses from the data generated by the experience, (4) developing a new course of action as a result of the experience, and (5) applying the new learning from the experience in real-world situations. This happens at both the group and individual levels of knowledge. David Kolb (1984, 105) says that "there are two kinds of knowledge: *personal knowledge,* the combination of my direct apprehensions of experience and the socially acquired comprehensions I use to explain this experience and guide my actions; and *social knowledge,* the independent, socially and culturally transmitted network of words, symbols and images that is based solely on comprehension."

Besides personal and social knowledge, theorists in this field often distinguish between *explicit* and *tacit* knowledge (Polanyi 1974). Explicit or declarative knowledge can be written down and transferred through direct instruction and memorization. Tacit knowledge is much harder to verbalize and is learned through bodily actions and experiences. Griffy-Brown and Hamlin (2003) note that "tacit knowledge is much more difficult than explicit knowledge to transfer and is usually learned personally and informally. Furthermore, tacit knowledge is usually a large part of business operations and critical for success. Surprisingly, this is true even in technical areas such as information systems that often change rapidly."

Online learning technologies that use text such as e-mail, chat, and discussion forums are less than ideal for learning, especially learning about the actions and reactions of others. There is a poverty of information because the amount of data available from the other person in an online conversation is minimal. The use of virtual worlds somewhat restores the balance by giving us more signals about what a person is thinking as well as a mutual recognition that we are communicating with a real person. This feeling is known as "telepresence."

Experiential learning (also known as "learning by doing") has been studied and written about for a long time. The American philosopher John Dewey, in a 1938 book entitled *Experience and Education*, said that "all genuine education comes from experience." Such experience is always located in a context or environment. Dewey (1938) wrote, "An experience is always what it is because of a transaction taking place between an individual and what, at that time, constitutes his environment."

Dewey's emphasis on experience for learning was reinforced by Kurt Lewin, a social psychologist who wrote about the environment as a "lifespace" and the "interdependence" of each person with those others in his or her environment (Lewin 1936). In creating a virtual world we are developing a new lifespace or learning environment in order to interact with others. Recently, neuroscience has shown that we develop empathy for others through using "mirror neurons" that allow us to experience in our imaginations what others are going through. The presence of an avatar allows us to connect in our minds much more readily to others than we would in situations where we are communicating only through the use of text.

Luckner and Nadler (1997) support the effectiveness of team-based experiential learning, citing the following factors:

▶ **Equality.** Experience tends to level the playing field as all participants share a common but novel experience.

▶ **Development of relationships.** Participants working on new and unfamiliar projects tend to develop as a team and through strengthening of individual relationships.

▶ **Disequilibrium.** New challenges tend to create a sense of instability that then allows new learning to take place.

▶ **Projection of inner self.** Members of a team tend to project their personalities and personal styles while working on a task. Often this projection is unconscious, revealing much about each person as they work with others on the task.

▶ **Increased speed of decision making.** Working together on a challenge can reduce caution and increase the ability of group members to move forward on decision making and task completion.

▶ **Meta learning.** Groups working together often stop and evaluate what they are doing, or review what they have done as part of the exercise.

▶ **Creation of a safe environment while encouraging risk taking.** Experiential learning tasks usually have built-in safety factors that limit the risk of failure. In fact, failure can be a positive part of the learning process as participants are encouraged to move out of their "comfort zones."

▶ **Embodiment of learning.** Experiential learning involves the body in learning through the senses and bodily actions, leaving a "kinesthetic imprint" that strengthens the memory of what is learned.

▶ **Shared narrative.** A learning experience provides a common language and stories for the members of the group. These new narratives can be helpful in spreading what was learned to others in the organization.

▶ **Range of roles.** Team tasks allow participants to try on different roles and to learn about the diversity of strengths within a group.

Experience by itself is not learning but must be connected to other processes for it to be successful. Jacques Lacan (1977) says that "individual development arises from the relationship between need, internalized representation, self-identification, and social interaction." Carl Rogers (1969), the famous therapist, presents four principles of experiential learning that demonstrate that it is a set of interconnected processes:

1. Significant learning takes place when the subject matter is relevant to the personal interests of the student.
2. Learning that is threatening to the self (e.g., new attitudes or perspectives) is more easily assimilated when external threats are at a minimum.
3. Learning proceeds faster when the threat to the self is low.
4. Self-initiated learning is the most lasting and pervasive.

Finally, and most recently, Donald Schön's (1995) theory of experiential learning draws on many of the perspectives of those who came before him. His theory was developed out of a series of case studies he did on professionals in architecture, psychotherapy, engineering, scientific research, town planning, and business management. Later he added education to the list of programs that he studied. Schön says that learning continues to take place after an experience through "reflective practices."

This raises the issue of the role of the instructor in experiential learning. Simply having experiences without guidance or reflection is not optimal, argues Kirschner et al. (2006). In a highly controversial article entitled, "Why minimal guidance during instruction does not work: An analysis of the failure of constructivist, discovery, problem-based, experiential, and inquiry-based teaching," they argue that "direct instruction" works better than all of the approaches that they list in their title. Their critics replied in the April 2007 issue of *Educational Psychologist* that Kirschner and his colleagues did not understand that all these approaches are not identical, and that there is a facilitation role for instructors in most instances where these "nondirective" approaches to training are used. That is, the role of the instructor in experiential learning is *not* to provide direct instruction to students but to help them to take risks, work through conflicts and other difficulties, and reflect on the experience after it is over.

There is a wide variety of approaches to experiential learning presently being used in employee training. These include:

► **Live training exercises in circumstances as realistic as possible.** This is the traditional approach to experiential learning—setting up an environment that replicates the situations that trainees might be in, and having them perform to the best of their abilities. This approach is used in training for firefighters, live fire training in the army, and simulations of large-scale disasters. In some cases, such as training in medical diagnostics, live actors are used to simulate patients or other roles. This type of training is very expensive, is often risky, or can't be carried out for ethical reasons.

► **Simulations that use special equipment.** In order to reduce risk, some training situations use special simulators in place of more expensive equipment or where risks make live training impossible. Examples include training to fly airplanes, maintain nuclear reactors, or practice surgery. In these cases, expensive complex simulators try to create as realistic a simulation as possible without the risks to humans or the environment.

► **Learning games.** Games can be used for training both in real-world environments and online. Games are seen to provide psychological benefits, particularly in motivating younger workers to get involved with the tasks of their workplace. Games are seen as engaging, even addicting. Recent research has also supported the hypothesis that games seem to improve learning in general. James Paul Gee (2006) answers the question, "Are video games good for learning?" with these six benefits:

1. Video games can create an embodied empathy for a complex system.
2. They are simulations of embodied experience and preparation for action.
3. They involve distributed intelligence via the creation of smart tools.
4. They create opportunities for cross-functional affiliation.

5. They allow meanings to be situated.
6. They can be open ended in ways that encourage a melding of personal and social goals.

Although there are only a few empirical studies of the impact of learning games in business environments, the studies that exist show a positive effect on motivation, morale, and learning outcomes. In their new book *Changing the Game: How Video Games Are Transforming the Future of Business,* Edery and Mollick (2009) state that games work in the workplace because they are entertaining (and therefore motivating), have great interactivity, and end up with learners immersed in the problems presented by the game.

▶ **Collaborative projects.** Collaborative training projects can be considered a form of experiential learning since they often involve hands-on experiences in problem solving, interacting with peers, and building knowledge together. This can be done through live meetings and events, Web conferencing, teleconferencing, and using purpose-built "computer-supported collaborative learning" (CSCL) software systems.

People may not even realize they are engaged in collaborative learning or that they are making a contribution to building knowledge for themselves and others. For example, the small actions of many people adding "bookmarks" on the World Wide Web can result in building knowledge assets that can be used by everyone. These sites are all examples of user-generated content and the development of tagging systems by ordinary folks (hence, these tag collections are sometimes called "folksonomies").

Part of the challenge in making collaborative learning work in a corporate setting may be the competitive nature of most workplaces. Individuals compete with each other for increased pay and better positions, and companies compete with each other for more market share and better revenues. These factors may work against collaborative learning in the workplace.

Traditionally, computer-supported collaborative learning has been advanced as a solution when there is a high demand for innovation and coping with rapid change. Computers are useful in this situation for recording and analyzing processes of learning and can be used to make the collective thoughts of a group visible to members. Once visible, these thoughts can be shared, reflected upon, and modified by participants (Woodill 2008).

▶ **Virtual worlds.** Virtual worlds are just starting to be used as a venue for experiential learning. In the next section, we discuss some of the most important uses of virtual worlds in business, especially as applied to employee training.

Enterprise Applications of Virtual Worlds

Training, or specifically designed employee learning, is only one of many business applications of virtual worlds. Informal learning can take place through many different activities, so it is best to review how virtual worlds can be used in enterprise settings today (in the last chapter of the book we look at some of the possible future uses of virtual worlds). We see five major areas where virtual worlds are used already or can be used in the corporate world:

1. corporate training
2. recruiting and new-hire orientation
3. team building and leadership training
4. enterprise collaboration
5. commerce, marketing, and other applications

Let us review these areas in more detail.

Corporate Training

Corporate trainers are starting to use virtual worlds in a variety of interesting ways, including direct instruction, training simulations, language immersion, diversity training, procedural practice, and the visualization of complex situations.

DIRECT INSTRUCTION. One way training in virtual worlds happens is direct instruction, with virtual lecture halls, theaters, and classrooms. Avatars are often used to simulate large lectures by being at the front of a virtual space, with rows of avatars sitting in chairs "listening" to the lecture. There are meeting rooms for tutorials and offices for instructors. In other words, it is a reproduction of the real environment of a typical university, college, or training facility.

TRAINING SIMULATIONS. Another way that training happens in virtual worlds is through training simulations, which is very different from the virtual lecture approach and probably more effective as a teaching method. Environments are constructed so that the learner experiences what it is like to operate in a certain situation in the real world. For example, the Canadian Border Services Agency trains border guards at a community college in a virtual world that simulates a border-crossing environment, where trainees, through their avatars, get to question and challenge avatars representing people trying to cross the border between Canada and the United States.

There are other examples of simulations for emergency responses and for crises in business situations. Some of these simulations and online games are good ways to support leadership training. What can you learn in these situations? Many things, according to Charles Nebolsky et al. (2003), including:

► communication
► situational awareness and flexibility

- ▶ intelligent risk-taking
- ▶ envisioning the future
- ▶ planning
- ▶ team organization
- ▶ process management
- ▶ crisis management
- ▶ conflict resolution
- ▶ team motivation

LANGUAGE IMMERSION AND DIVERSITY TRAINING. Virtual worlds seem ideal for training in how to speak other languages or how to act in unfamiliar cultures or situations. Immersion in other languages and cultures populated by native speakers is a great way to practice skills in close-to-real situations. For example, Garcia-Ruiz et al. (2008) describe the implementation of a wireless virtual reality environment for Mexican engineering students to practice comprehension of English. Furthermore, by using immersive virtual reality, anyone can experience the world as another person and explore what it is like to be a person with a different gender, social status, race, or body. Fresh et al. (2008) review the use of 3-D multiuser virtual environments (MUVEs) to simulate experiences in foreign cultures and suggest that "intercultural competence is a necessity for the successful negotiation of cross-cultural situations."

PROCEDURAL PRACTICE. Procedural practice involves learning the correct sequence of actions in order to perform a particular task. The task may be as simple as routing a lost traveler to the correct area of the airport, or as complex as preparing a patient for the surgery. Virtual worlds are perfect for this kind of training, since they allow the trainee to perform the procedures in an environment closely resembling real life, receive immediate feedback during the process, and practice the procedure until it is performed almost automatically. As demonstrated by the case study of the University of Kansas Medical Center (see Chapter 10), procedural training in virtual worlds helps trainees to separate physical knowledge ("how to") and process knowledge ("why and in what order").

This helps to reduce cognitive load and improves the efficiency and quality of training.

VISUALIZATION OF COMPLEX SITUATIONS. Virtual worlds can be used to visualize and learn about complex adaptive systems such as human societies or enterprise architecture. They are able to accurately represent the complexity of real-life environments and situations. The example of Michelin (see the case study in Chapter 7) demonstrates that by using a visualization of complexity, Second Life training succeeded where all other existing methods failed. Modeling within virtual worlds can also be used to study such phenomena as the outbreak and spread of diseases. Clark Quinn (2008) sees virtual worlds as laboratories for the application of "systems thinking." Such thinking, says Quinn, is "part of a new skill set we need to have, and spatial modeling and using spatial representations gives us an extra representation dimension to comprehend and communicate." This shift to 3-D visualization is about seeing and doing rather than reading about something.

Recruiting and New-Hire Orientation

For a company with many locations, using a virtual world is an inexpensive and effective way to gather and interview new recruits and to introduce them to company operations.

RECRUITING AND RETENTION OF EMPLOYEES. Faced with competition for technically skilled workers, organizations are turning to virtual worlds as recruiting vehicles. For example, the Vancouver police have used Second Life to hold recruiting sessions (Leung 2007). Recruiting in virtual worlds especially makes sense for technology companies, but it doesn't stop there. For example, TMP was the first company to set up a recruiting service in Second Life for companies in different industry sectors, and global consulting company Accenture has built a Careers Island in Second Life (Driver 2008).

NEW-HIRE ORIENTATION. An important new use of virtual worlds is their potential role in hiring, orientation, and training. It is especially important as retiring baby boomers are replaced with generation Y employees, who have lived all their lives with information technology. Classroom lectures are not enough on their own to capture Generation Y's attention and leverage their high levels of ambition and enthusiasm. The ability to run new-hire orientation programs for employees in different locations, as well as asynchronously, contributes to the appeal of expanding new-hire orientation into the virtual worlds.

Team Building and Leadership Training

A study on using a virtual world for "team training" showed that students were able to learn their roles in a team task as well as how to coordinate their actions with their teammates (Rickel and Johnson 1999). Virtual humans were able to serve as instructors for individual students or as substitutes for missing team members. In another study (Heinrichs et al. 2008), individuals in clinical training programs concerned with critical medical care learned to manage clinical cases effectively as members of a virtual team, whereas practice on live patients can't be well controlled and doesn't offer the same variety of possible medical conditions that can be simulated in a virtual world medical setting, especially for rare diseases.

There are also some negatives expressed by learners in the use of a virtual world such as Second Life as a teamwork learning environment. A study by Trotta and Mirliss (2007) showed that one barrier to the use of virtual worlds is that students don't see them as educational spaces because they are not like classrooms. Comments from students included:

- ► "The environment is more like a game than an educational setting."
- ► "While Second Life is interesting, it is too open to the public and things can be detrimental."
- ► "People in Second Life are not normal."
- ► "Computers have too large a part in our lives."

In spite of these conservative reactions, team-building exercises and games in virtual worlds are becoming increasingly popular. The important factor in adoption of virtual worlds for teamwork training is the ability to objectively record, store, and process data on each team and team member's performance (see Chapter 8 for details), versus only observation by an instructor in a real-world teamwork exercise.

Enterprise Collaboration

Increasingly, staff members in large organizations are required to collaborate with each other in many kinds of tasks but may be separated by significant geographical distances. Meeting in a virtual world brings everyone on a team together in one place. Following are some of the ways that collaboration can happen using a virtual world.

MEETING SPACES. Virtual worlds have become places to hold meetings of all sorts, from a one-on-one discussion to a virtual conference. Educational institutions, religious groups, and many companies have constructed virtual spaces for meetings. One problem with virtual meeting spaces is that their designers often concentrate on creating exact replicas of real-world meeting rooms, failing to take advantage of the unique features of virtual world spaces that give them their advantages. It might be more productive to create virtual meeting spaces as they did at MIT to "take full advantage of the features that set it apart both from other mediated environments and real-world meeting rooms," such as the ability of virtual rooms to record and map the flow of ideas in the conversations that are taking place (Naone 2007). One additional advantage of virtual meeting spaces is the significant reduction in travel costs for staff and the costs of renting space in the real world.

COLLABORATION ON PROJECTS. Virtual worlds are spaces for collaboration. One of the areas "natural" for collaboration is the use of virtual worlds in architectural design (Kieran 2007). Collaboration is the objective of the Croquet Project, a new open source operating system that has been designed for deep collaboration between teams in virtual worlds. Until recently little systematic study has been carried out in controlled experiments that would support use of collaboration in a virtual world (Kahai et al. 2007). However, the latest research demonstrates that collaboration in virtual worlds does improve team performance (Massey and Montoya 2008 and TechRadar 2008; see Chapter 12 for more details).

COLLECTIVE INTELLIGENCE. Virtual worlds have the potential to be used for both political organizing and for the re-creation of political spaces, such as legislatures. Roy Mark (2007) describes how Second Life has been used for "virtual lobbying," and Nancy Scola (2007) sees "avatar politics" as a way of mobilizing youth to become involved in the political process.

Virtual spaces can be used to further collective decision making. A university in Amsterdam is conducting an experiment with 240 business administration students to see if a virtual world such as Second Life can be used as a "decision support system" (Van den Hooff 2009).

Commerce, Marketing, and Other Applications

While the focus of this book is on the use of virtual worlds for human resources functions such as training, recruiting, and orientation, there are many other uses for virtual worlds in businesses.

COMMERCE. Virtual worlds are places where business can be conducted live and online. There is a lot of marketing, buying, and selling taking place in virtual worlds that goes on every day, and this virtual economy will continue to grow. Early in the life of Second Life, stories abounded about individuals who were making a good living "in-world," selling virtual real estate and virtual clothing, which resulted in a "gold rush" mentality, driving thousands of people to offer goods for sale in Second Life.

INFORMATION SOURCES. Virtual worlds such as Second Life are home to many information providers who are happy to have visitors access their materials. For example, several countries have opened embassies in Second Life, providing materials on immigration and answering inquiries. The Library of Congress has held exhibits of its vast holdings in Second Life. The Alliance Library System started its Second Life location in 2006, hosting audiobooks and exhibits. Now there are more than forty other libraries in the Info Island Archipelago in Second Life (Townsend-Gard and Arnold 2008).

CUSTOMER SERVICE. Visitors to virtual worlds can receive assistance and support from companies that have set up service booths. Virtual agents in the form of robotic avatars can answer questions, or the booth can be staffed by an avatar controlled by a live person. At a minimum, these spaces allow links to a company website where further information is available. Referring to Second Life specifically, *BusinessWeek* stated that "the virtual world could become the first point of contact between companies and customers and could transform the whole experience" (Best 2007).

SUPPORT, ADVICE, AND THERAPY. Need help for personal problems or a support group for divorced singles? Many groups have been set up in virtual worlds for you to join and find the support you need. For example, Contact a Family, a charity that helps parents of children with disabilities, has set up a virtual office in Second Life. There are dozens of other support and therapy groups in Second Life, ranging from groups for people with Asperger's syndrome to counseling for HIV/AIDS (Norris 2009).

NEW REALITIES AND PERSPECTIVES. Virtual worlds offer new ways of interacting with the world and with others. Walk-throughs and fly-throughs of constructed environments (where avatars walk or fly within a virtual environment) provide new perspectives and the emergence of new behaviors, such as "griefing"—messing up someone else's experience in a virtual world. Of course, virtual worlds can provide the setting for reconstructions of real-world environments and events, which can be useful in presenting history or evidence in criminal cases. Alternative scenarios can be presented and replayed. In addition, unique environments that do not and perhaps cannot exist in the real world allow participants alternative ways of being that are unique to virtual settings.

VIRTUAL WORLDS AS RESEARCH SITES. Virtual worlds are places where people come together, so it is not surprising that they are also seen as valuable research sites. Focus groups can be created in-world that target specific populations. The behavior of avatars can also be studied and recorded. One group has even developed a set of educational research and evaluation data collection procedures for Second Life (Sherman and Tillies 2007).

VIRTUAL WORLDS AS RECREATION AND SOCIAL SITES. Virtual worlds are places where people also go to relax, have fun, and meet other people. While this may not be seen as employee training, it may be an important aspect of employee health, welfare, and morale. Second Life, for example, has numerous performance spaces for live entertainment and sports, gaming environments, art galleries, and other cultural venues. Meeting spaces for social networking abound in Second Life and are a compelling reason why many people go in-world in the first place.

The Competitive Advantages of Virtual Worlds

The many advantages of using virtual worlds in business come from the unique "affordances" (qualities that allow something to happen) that virtual worlds provide. Here are some of the many things that you can do in a virtual world:

► **Immersive and unique experiences.** In a virtual world, learners are immersed in a 3-D world where things can happen that are not possible in the real world.

- **Trying another role.** In a virtual world, you can try on a particular role or persona that you don't have in real life.
- **Problem-based learning.** Virtual worlds allow instructional designers to set up problems to be solved by learners. For example, just learning to build within a virtual world environment is a problem-solving activity in itself.
- **Assessments.** Virtual worlds are places to observe others to see how well they perform a task or answer a question.
- **Collaboration.** Because many people can work and play together in the same virtual space, virtual worlds are ideal for collaboration.
- **Learning spaces.** Virtual worlds can be places where one can learn from both doing and listening, and where instruction and apprenticeships can take place.

Virtual worlds have so many benefits for enterprises that want to stay on the leading edge of development, that not at least experimenting with them can put an organization at a serious competitive disadvantage. Tony O'Driscoll (2007) at Duke University speaks of the "seven sensibilities of virtual social worlds" that can confer major benefits for companies employing virtual worlds. The seven sensibilities are:

- The sense of self—you are your avatar
- The death of distance—you can teleport to any place in a fraction of a second
- The power of presence—interacting with others, sense of being with others
- The sense of space—3-D movement; physical barriers can feel real
- The capability to co-create—creative peer production
- The pervasiveness of practice—"How do I . . . ?" training through practice with simulations
- The enrichment of experience—the augmentation of experience and opening of new possibilities

These seven sensibilities, and others, add up to providing an increased sense of engagement for learners in virtual worlds. Through virtual worlds, the participant or learner becomes a character in a narrative as it unfolds or is created. Learning in virtual environments feels authentic; that is, learners seem to be willing to suspend disbelief and relate to virtual reality as if it was the real world. The experience is so authentic that learners often develop and maintain complex dynamic social relationships with other users.

Increased engagement can also result from having the right mix of learning technologies that fit with the various generational cohorts found within a given workplace. Training expectations and experiences of baby boomers can be quite different from those of the "millennial" generation. With baby boomers reaching between forty-six and sixty-five in 2010, the need to focus on the ideal ways of engaging younger workers is important.

The sense of authenticity is further enhanced by the extended range of virtual world spaces. There is a "network effect" involved here—the more users there are, the more interesting the virtual world is, as possibilities and spaces expand with each additional user. In the case of Second Life, this reach is global, and the experience of the world is one of many languages, cultures, and behaviors. Persons with a variety of disabilities see Second Life as a "level playing field," where they are represented by their avatar, not by their disability.

The fact that virtual worlds usually have many of the same persistent characteristics of the physical world that everyone knows is a real advantage. Training in how to navigate through a virtual world is usually very simple. Philip Rosedale, founder of Second Life, says, "Virtual worlds are inherently comprehensible to us in a way that the Web is not . . . they look like the world we already know and take advantage of our ability to remember and organize. . . . Information is presented there in a way that matches our memories and experiences. . . . [The] ability to remember the words we use and the information we talk about is much higher if it's presented as a room or space around us."

Employing a virtual world environment for training can also dramatically decrease the cost and improve the availability of training. Training can be spread out throughout a long period of time as the virtual world can be an ongoing channel of information and practice, available 24/7. Learners can be in multiple locations at the same time, and the training setup can be easily repeated.

Compared to alternative technologies, deploying virtual worlds is far less expensive. For example, videoconferencing systems with "telepresence" are very pricey, require installation of hardware in every office, and still often require employees to visit a separate studio away from their normal workplace. Telepresence is important to maintaining a sense of engagement, and this is where virtual worlds have an advantage over ordinary Web experiences. On a website people are anonymous and invisible, while in a virtual world they are represented by a moving avatar with lifelike qualities. This seems to make a big difference to users in terms of the believability of the experience and their connection with others.

It is difficult to train for many situations, due to high risk or the high costs of using a working environment for training rather than production. With a "virtual sandbox" there are lower risks resulting from failure or bad decisions. This fact is very important in such fields as medicine, military training, or the operation of nuclear reactors. In fact, some of the training that can be provided in a virtual world is simply not feasible in the physical world.

Finally, virtual worlds can be a great environment to enhance and maintain a company's brand. By creating experimental worlds to support enthusiasts for their product or brand, companies can increase the "stickiness" (the amount of time that a person spends interacting with a particular product or brand) of their principal customer groups.

 ## Problems and Issues with Virtual Worlds

A 2008 report by the consulting firm Forrester, titled "Getting Real Work Done in Virtual Worlds," notes that in spite of all the potential benefits of virtual worlds, the tools for development are not "user friendly." "You've practically got to be a gamer to use most of these tools," Forrester concludes. This state of affairs has been improving as the field matures, and it represents a business opportunity for a growing number of enterprising companies that are developing improved tools for virtual worlds. The Forrester report also states that virtual worlds such as Second Life, There.com, and "more business-focused offerings" are emerging as valuable work tools. (Driver et al. 2008)

While we are enthusiastic about the potential of the use of virtual worlds in business environments, it is important to note some of the problems and issues associated with them. Some of the problems are a lack of acceptance of virtual worlds as being a serious place to learn. As often happens with new technologies, this is especially true for older executives who often see virtual worlds as frivolous places to "play games."

The learning curve for virtual worlds can be quite steep; sometimes four to six hours are needed to learn the basic navigation of the environment and how to build objects and change the characteristics of avatars. Real mastery of a virtual world usually takes much longer. Based on the successful projects of Michelin, the University of Kansas, and others, we can suggest limiting training to essential virtual world features needed in the simulation and avoiding less relevant items, such as creating and customizing an avatar. Pre-creating avatars for learners so that they do not spend instruction time opening accounts or customizing avatars also helps in eliminating many "learning curve"–type problems.

The building of objects and environments is limited by technology and may not be as realistic or accurate as one might wish. Recent introduction of sculptured prims (short for "primitives"—basic building blocks in Second Life) technology reduces this problem to a minimum. Sculptured prims technology allows you to create objects in popular 3-D modeling programs, such as Blender, 3D Max, Maya, or Wings 3D, and upload them to Second Life. Use of sculptured prims gives designers an opportunity to build rather precise and sophisticated models, although this precision comes at the expense of time and effort.

As a new type of public space, virtual worlds raise issues that are unique and can be troublesome. For residents of some virtual worlds, this new space can seem like the "Wild West" where "anything goes" without constraints. Like all human endeavors, issues of law, ethics, etiquette, design, and money can raise their heads. Issues of the "presentation of self," maintaining an image, sharing spaces, negotiating roles, and building confidence and trust all need to be dealt with in virtual worlds. Thinking ahead, following suitable access and security policies, and working with the community at large help minimize or eliminate these issues, as shown by the examples of Intel, Microsoft, EMC, and other companies.

"Outward"-oriented projects (projects targeting people outside your organization) carry additional challenges that need to be addressed for a project to be successful. You often need to put significant effort toward building a community. Forming and maintaining persistent social groups is not easy in a virtual world because users must log back in to find each other and have a set of common tasks, environmental features, and objects with which to work or play. Leadership can be an issue for setting up, maintaining, and running social groups within virtual worlds, which are often structured around the idea of "guilds" or apprenticeships to an expert. "Managing a guild, however, is notoriously difficult and many do not survive very long" (Ducheneaut et al. 2007).

In virtual worlds there is potential confusion and distraction caused by dealing with dual identities both for oneself and with others. This can be both good and bad suggests Chris Dede of Harvard University in 1995:

Some types of participants who are attracted to virtual communities (e.g. people denying unpleasant aspects of reality; people who present a persona to the world radically different than their internal self-image) are likely to have suboptimal learning behaviors as well. Synthetic constructivist environments provide a safe, anonymous opportunity to experiment with a new persona centered on a learning-centered lifestyle. For example, a person who feels ashamed of "being wrong"—and therefore is frightened of learning-by-doing situations—while masked within the context of a virtual community can safely risk making mistakes in the process of learning.

Being able to disguise one's identity can lead to a lack of inhibition for behaviors that a person would not dare to exhibit in the real world. Some people, known as "griefers," take pleasure in messing up the virtual world experiences and destroying the online creations of others. The good way to prevent this in a corporate environment is to control access to your location(s), closing areas that are intended for internal corporate use to the general public, just as you would create password-protected areas on your website.

Because of the large amount of bandwidth and personal computer power required for virtual worlds, to use them successfully learners usually need newer computers with a fast video card. Some organizations create a separate "virtual world" classroom with newer computers where employees can get access to virtual worlds, instead of updating a significant number of computers simultaneously. Human resources or the marketing department can also use these computers for their projects. With our experience of how fast computer technology catches up with the requirements of new software, we can venture a guess that this is a temporary solution that might not be needed by the time you read this book or soon thereafter.

Another potential problem that you might want to consider is that the architecture of many virtual worlds limits the number of concurrent users in any given region. Although this number is increasing as virtual world technology matures, you always need to take into consideration the limit that exists in your virtual world of choice and plan your projects accordingly.

 ## The Challenges Ahead

What does this all mean for a trainer or instructional designer trying to set up educational opportunities within a virtual world environment? It means that virtual worlds can be a challenging environment, especially for those training personnel who are used to working with employees in more traditional ways. In order to be successful in a virtual world, they need to develop a set of technical skills, acquire new leadership strategies, and have a solid knowledge of how virtual worlds work. They also may be dealing with learners who are not experienced with a virtual world environment, or with learners who do not have the requisite network connections or computing facilities.

Virtual worlds are still at an early stage of development. As they become more accepted and used in corporate environments, you can expect that both the quantity and quality of development tools for these new environments will rapidly increase.

Virtual Worlds:
Selecting the Best

by the time you reach this chapter, you have probably realized that the authors are not impartial observers of virtual worlds but rather passionate supporters of their use in the corporate world. There are already numerous success stories—some of which are presented as case studies later in the book—showing that training, collaboration, recruiting, and even marketing benefit from a carefully planned program that uses virtual worlds as a platform. We would love you to get into a virtual world as soon as possible and try it yourself.

> "I am easily satisfied with the very best."
> —*Winston Churchill*

There is one dilemma, though: as of this writing, the virtualworlds review.com website lists twenty-nine (!) virtual worlds. We can add quite a few not mentioned in the list, bringing the total of virtual world platforms available today to more than forty. How do you navigate this list? The virtual worlds listed are categorized in groups such as "Best for Kids," "Best for 40+," "Best for Artists," "Best for Broadband Connection," and similar ones. However, there are no categories that would indicate applicability for business use. There is no "Best for Fortune 100," "Best for Big Pharma,"

"Best for Midsized Business," "Best for Sales Training," or "Best for Technical Training" in the list. This leaves the question, "Which virtual world platform would work best in a corporate environment?" wide open.

The situation does not become any easier when you consider that virtual worlds can serve as a platform for many dissimilar purposes. The authors of this book do not know your plans, requirements, corporate culture, background, and other factors, so we probably cannot pinpoint the "correct" choice (if there would be only one "correct" choice!). Still, we can review major alternatives you have, suggest issues you might want to consider, and help you narrow your selection.

Virtual Worlds—a General Picture

Perhaps the most obvious classification of the virtual worlds is based on the way you see them. There are virtual worlds that operate inside a regular Web browser, such as Internet Explorer or Firefox, and there are virtual worlds that require downloading and installation of a special program that works as your window into the virtual world. This program is called a "client program," or simply, "the client."

Your first instinct probably tells you that the browser-based virtual worlds have an advantage. You do not need to download and install additional software, which in a corporate environment is a serious task in itself, probably requiring that you get permission from the information technology (IT) department. Moreover, the fact that these virtual worlds work in a Web browser means that you are likely to be able to reach them from your corporate network, just as you would open a regular website for viewing. This makes it easier to get a green light from IT, which can be a very attractive consideration for some corporate users.

However, this convenience comes at a price. Virtual worlds in this group can provide only cartoonlike settings and characters, a far cry from the realistically immersive environments created by specialized clients. Your ability to customize browser-based environments, or to create and modify objects you need for training—such as models of equipment, or even a screen to show slides or a movie—are limited at best. Creation of training simulations, especially automated simulations that trainees can use at their discretion, integration of virtual world training with existing live and distance learning programs, or integration with your learning management system are practically impossible. There are very few outside developers who work with browser-based virtual worlds. Building the new training modules and adding changes and modifications to existing training units typically must be completed by the platform vendor.

If this gives you pause, consider another factor: communication is the *single* strong feature of browser-based virtual worlds, and even in this area they are not exactly business- or training-friendly. You can exchange text messages and, at least in some cases, use voice. However, for business applications you need the ability to share visuals, record and replay conversations, and exchange data. These capabilities are largely missing in browser-based virtual worlds. Their features are consumer-oriented, making them especially popular among (and oftentimes targeted toward) preteens and teens, which is reflected even in their names: "Barbie Girls," "Club Penguin," "Papermint," "Zwinktopia." Perhaps the most famous browser-based virtual world—and the one with the promise to reach beyond teenage demographics—was Google's Lively. It became available on July 8, 2008. Unfortunately, Google discontinued the "experiment in providing people with more ways to express themselves" (Lively 2008) less than half a year later, on December 31, 2008. The slogan about people expressing themselves might well outlive Lively as a generic description of a browser-based virtual world.

Active Worlds is an interesting "transitional" platform. It has a stand-alone client that supports Web browsing, similar to a regular Web browser such as Internet Explorer or Firefox (Figure 3.1).

In addition to Web and 3-D virtual world browsing, Active Worlds supports voice chat and basic instant messaging. Paying users, called

FIGURE 3.1

"citizens" in the Active Worlds lingo, and "world owners" (as opposed to "tourists"—nonpaying users) can create their own environment with custom content.

There is a rather intricate system of rights in Active Worlds, but, generally speaking, the platform provides instruments for creation of custom content and very limited scripting. Active Worlds was one of the first platforms to make its software development kit (SDK) available, which allows software developers and advanced users to extend platform capabilities and build their own worlds.

Very innovative and useful for business purposes is a user's ability to create *bots* (as in ro*bots*—an avatar that inhabits a virtual world and interacts with users, but which is driven by a computer program instead of a human being) using the Active Worlds SDK. Bots allow users to automate various tasks. In corporate training contexts, bots can be used to play the role of a patient in a nurses' training, the role of receptionist or purchasing manager in sales training, or the role of an angry customer or a difficult coworker in communications training. They can be used to offer introduction and policy explanations as a part of new-hire orientation, provide a tour of a facility, administer a test on using equipment, and complete many other tasks.

Now, note the word *can* in the previous sentences. We are not aware of anybody actually using bots in Active Worlds for these purposes. In fact, while several educational organizations still support their Active Worlds installations and have not migrated to other virtual worlds due to budget considerations (Virtual Social Worlds and Libraries blog 2007), to our knowledge, there is no active corporate presence in Active Worlds. Our opinion of what *can* be done is based on what *is being* done in a different virtual world (Second Life, see Chapter 9). The ideas behind Active Worlds are great, but their implementation feels clunky and dated, as if the software languished for a long time with little development. It does not have a cohesive immersive feeling characteristic of modern 3-D platforms. Perhaps you can find a more advanced choice for your virtual world project.

Most virtual worlds—especially those that realistically can be used in corporate environments for training and collaboration—use their own client program. When considering virtual worlds for these purposes it is important to look beyond the technicalities and establish your objectives and priorities.

All virtual worlds encourage communication. However, in many of them, social networking and communication components outweigh other uses to such a degree that the virtual worlds are thought of and used almost exclusively as social networking tools. Perhaps the best-known advanced virtual world in this group is There.com (Figure 3.2). It is a hosted application—you download a client and use it to connect to a server located on the vendor's network. There.com includes facilities for chat and "private chat"—essentially, instant messaging that allows you to include/exclude participants in the conversation. Voice capability is also available for an additional fee. You will always be able to hear other users, but unless you purchase voice capabilities you will be limited to typing text when you want to say something. Finally, you can also create your own movies and post them for anyone to see—a useful feature in training.

Still, the features outside text and voice communication provided by the social networking group of virtual worlds are either basic or absent. We are talking about such critical items as security, access control, intellectual property control, creation and modeling of custom equipment and environments, and access to scripting. In the absence of such features, these virtual worlds are hardly usable in corporate training or business collaboration, in spite of their capabilities in supporting social interactions.

 ## Virtual World Selection Criteria

In general, our experience in building, programming, and organizing events in a virtual world provides the basis for the list of what normally must be available in a virtual world for corporate (and many academic) clients to feel comfortable and consider it for their training and other business needs:

FIGURE 3.2

▶ **Reliability.** The virtual world should have accessible technical support, either from the original vendor or from the third-party consultants and developers.

▶ **Security.** The virtual world should have the ability to protect private information and intellectual property (IP).

▶ **Vendor stability.** As with any other endeavor, you want to be sure that a virtual world you select is supported by a stable, dependable organization.

► **Scalability.** The size of your organization and projected usage for both a pilot phase and normal use will certainly be a factor in your selection.

► **Advanced access control and user privileges system.** The virtual world should include strict management of user activities and controlled access to your company's virtual location, simulations, and events. You absolutely want to make sure that the system is capable of providing high-granularity access control, in other words, you have precise control over who has access to what at what time.

► **A quality 3-D virtual environment.** The virtual world should have a high level of customizable graphics and customizable sophisticated avatars. Human behavior in virtual worlds and their acceptance are influenced, to a degree, by virtual worlds being a realistic environment. You probably want to avoid virtual worlds with a cartoonlike feeling and comic strip–like characters, as they tend not to encourage the kind of professional behavior that more lifelike ones will.

► **In-world creation/modeling/scripting tools.** These tools allow both fast prototyping and creation of sophisticated simulations. Ideally, your team should be able to quickly learn to use in-world creation tools for at least simple tasks. This will significantly speed up prototyping and communication between instructional designers and the developer team. At the same time, the tools should be sophisticated enough for developers to be able to create lifelike simulations, connect them to a database or a learning management system, and provide interconnectivity with existing Internet and intranet applications using encrypted and unencrypted connections.

► **Dependable multimodal communication methods.** The virtual world should include text, instant messages, voice, and secure communications. As demonstrated by Intel's experience (see Chapter 6), access to several modes of conversation fosters unique "multi-dimensional" simultaneous exchange, a valuable bonus in business communications that is not readily available outside virtual worlds.

▶ **Ability to connect to and exchange data with an outside database and/or learning management system.** Interconnectivity with existing training programs and business systems is critical in reaching the full potential of virtual world solutions, as well as acceptance of the new tools by your team.

There are two other parameters that, while they may not be absolutely critical for everybody, are of utmost importance to most companies looking to launch virtual world projects:

▶ **Extensive base of available developers, consultants, vendors of the complementary software, and customized solutions.** You are unlikely to find an "out-of-the-box" solution that precisely fits your needs, so the success of your project depends to a large degree on the availability of professionals who can help you. A large developer base can help you find appropriate experts for your situation. It is really advantageous (and a sign of a stable, established vendor) to find lists of developers who work with a certain virtual world solution on a vendor's website. Firstly, you can immediately see how deep is the bench and how diverse are the skills and experience you'll be counting on. Secondly, you can start interviewing developers in the very early stages of your decision-making process. Oftentimes, the information they will provide is more valuable than the sales pitch you will hear from a vendor.

▶ **Ability to import virtual world content created in third-party programs.** Programs such as 3D Studio Max, Blender, and other 3-D modeling and rendering programs allow you to build on the foundation of existing tools.

Finally, because virtual worlds are a highly visual environment, we would consider the following:

▶ **Ability to set up a tour to try a specific virtual world.** You may wish to see what others are doing, especially in your industry. A word of caution: do not expect to learn a lot from your competition's place in a virtual world, even if part of the virtual world's land is open to a general public. Just as you would not share your trade secrets and intellectual property with the competing organization, other companies keep the places where they conduct training and business meetings closed to outsiders. Recruiting, marketing, and other programs that are open to outsiders or are even targeted outward are usually located away from the intracompany-use areas that are closed to the public. You should be able, however, to see how easy or hard it is to operate in a particular virtual world, review tools that are available, and get a general "feel" for using the platform for your business needs.

There might be other factors specific to your organization, such as special hardware requirements or a particular platform or application you need supported, so be sure to make a list of those before you begin your evaluation.

Along with all the "must have" features, there are also parameters that you will generally try to avoid. In most cases, they are simply the opposite of the ones already listed. There is one additional elimination parameter that we can call *readiness*: sometimes you will find out that what people call a "virtual world" is in reality a collection of very basic server software and programming tools (called a software development kit, or SDK) that allow qualified programmers to build on that foundation, creating their own virtual worlds and experimenting with them.

The most notable of these SDK-type virtual worlds include Multiverse, Croquet, and Project Wonderland. Although they have excellent potential for later applications, these are not ready-to-use virtual worlds. Some of them, such as Multiverse, are commercial projects that base their income model on sharing revenue and/or royalty payments from developers who create multiuser online games. Others are open source and do not require revenue sharing but do not yet have an established user support system. In any event, unless you are in the software or technology business and are looking to create your own virtual world for your own use or as a source of revenue, you would be well advised to review other options.

 ## Enterprise-Friendly Virtual Worlds

Considering the requirements of ongoing business and the parameters we have discussed, a majority of virtual worlds can be eliminated based on a cursory review. Five virtual worlds that merit further detailed comparison and consideration are (in alphabetical order):

- ▶ Forterra OLIVE
- ▶ Open Simulator (OpenSim)
- ▶ ProtonMedia Protosphere
- ▶ Teleplace (formerly Qwaq)
- ▶ Second Life

Forterra Systems' OLIVE (www.forterrainc.com)

According to the Forterra's OLIVE product brochure, the "On-Line Interactive Virtual Environment (OLIVE) is a software platform that enables customers, partners, and developers to build persistent virtual worlds where users can collaborate over networks to communicate, train, rehearse, analyze, experiment, socialize, and entertain." The company stresses the availability of their software development kit, which "includes development and production tools, avatars and a range of options for 3-D content to rapidly create customized virtual environments ready for production." This SDK ostensibly allows customers to "create new types of distance learning, group collaboration solutions, and networked communities."

OLIVE is available in three configurations. In the core configuration you receive a basic server ("virtual island" or, simply, an "island" in virtual world lingo) and "a set of general 3D art assets including avatar clothing, gestures, faces, as well as buildings, vehicles, vegetation, and many other objects." Adding other features requires either licensing "functionality modules that extend the baseline capabilities of OLIVE" or "Content Packs consisting of sets of professionally developed 3D art assets, scenes and simulations. . . . Content Packs are available for First Responders, Medical, Meetings, Education, and Army/Infantry." Should you need a different or custom solution for your organization, Forterra offers SDK and three levels of nonproduction developer licenses (not to be used for developing products for sale)—basic, standard, and premium—to develop a 3-D application. (A developer license provides "the means to get trained, develop, test, demo, prototype and pilot a 3-D application with stake-holders before a production deployment.") (Reuters 2007)

You can also contract a third-party developer to work with you on customizing Forterra's solution, though the list of developers is not readily available on the company website, and it is unclear whether you can find, interview, and select a developer without the company's help.

The company promotes OLIVE as a virtual world that can be deployed on your network, behind a corporate firewall. Indeed, the ability to run an application on a corporate network is an important consideration if you plan to use the virtual world only internally. However, if you want to make your virtual world accessible outside the company, for example, in your recruiting effort or for collaboration between geographically dispersed teams, you have three alternative options (from easiest to hardest to implement): using a hosted service, running the server outside of the firewall, or opening specific ports in the corporate firewall. In order to review an OLIVE demo you need to contact the company by filling in an online form.

Forterra Systems, Inc. is located in San Mateo, California, and lists customers in the health care, government and defense, nonprofit, and education sectors (Forterra Systems 2008).

Open Simulator (www.opensimulator.org)

Open Simulator, better known as OpenSim, is a noncommercial open source project that was started by a group of virtual world enthusiasts in January of 2007. As a platform for operating a virtual world that can support multiple independent regions as a part of a single centralized grid, OpenSim is similar to Second Life (Figure 3.3). It can also run on a standalone server; for example, behind a corporate firewall. While started as an open source response to Second Life, OpenSim gradually developed its own identity. For example, in order to customize the behavior of objects, OpenSim supports most of the very basic Linden Script Language, a programming scripting language used to apply certain behavior to Second Life objects. On the other hand, along with Linden Script, OpenSim also uses more common computer-programming languages, such as C# (pronounced "see sharp") and its own OpenSim Scripting Language. These other languages are, however, incomplete in their virtual world implementation and noticeably less powerful than the scripting capabilities in Second Life.

In many regards, Open Simulator provides a blank slate that allows software developers to build their own virtual worlds. It is a promising project, but its "out-of-the-box" capabilities are more similar to a software developer kit than to a virtual world ready for corporate use.

ProtonMedia Protosphere (www.protonmedia.com)

ProtonMedia seems to be striving to provide an all-in-one business solution. Protosphere is an integrated platform that extends common social networking tools with the use of 3-D visualization (Figure 3.4). Similarly

FIGURE 3.3

FIGURE 3.4

to OLIVE, Protosphere can run a virtual world server behind a firewall. It also offers application sharing. Users not only can view the same documents in real time but can take turns changing them while at the same time communicating using voice or chat. Both voice and text chat are encrypted to ensure secure communications.

Because Protosphere also includes a whiteboard (a graphical area for drawing or writing) function, it can also work as a Web-conferencing tool. User profile management and search tools, as well as self-publishing, blog, and wiki capabilities, make it a social networking tool. Its built-in course launching and tracking capabilities are similar to those of a learning management system (LMS). Dedicated LMSs often have more functionality and might perform these tasks better, but the fact that Protosphere combines these features within one platform is very innovative and potentially useful. We like the fact that you can register on the company website and immediately download the demo version of the Protosphere client.

The social networking tools provided within the Protosphere platform are not "located" in a virtual world. These are pretty standard, though comprehensive, Web-based applications. The 3-D part of Protosphere seems to play a secondary role to ProtonMedia's vision of collaboration and social networking. The templates the company offers as an example of educational curriculum—"Fill in the Blank," "Line Matching," "True or False," and others—are the types of simple assessment tools that could be completed without any need to use a three-dimensional world.

Users' ability to build 3-D environments with Protosphere is limited (for example, users can create a conference room based on a template, but creating a fully customized room would require assistance from the vendor or an outside developer). The standard user interface does not include tools for building new objects, modeling their behavior, or scripting. You would have to contract the vendor or a developer to do that.

Developers who work with Protosphere are not listed on the company website. Moreover, Protosphere uses a relatively little-known computer language called Lua for scripting, which in itself limits the developer pool. In our opinion, the inability of users to readily build custom environments, create and use custom scripts, and create automated simulations may limit use of Protosphere in a corporate environment.

According to the company website (www.protonmedia.com), Proton-Media was established in 1998, is based in suburban Philadelphia, and has more than two dozen clients in pharmaceuticals, medical devices, financial services, and technology.

Teleplace (www.teleplace.com)

Teleplace (formerly Qwaq) provides virtual collaboration solutions using a 3-D environment as the foundation (Figure 3.5). In its functionality, Teleplace, or "Teleplace Multi-Share" (formerly "Quaq Forums") as the platform is known officially, is very similar to Protosphere, although it lacks some of the social networking tools of Protosphere, such as wikis and blogs. The tools that are present, in our opinion, have a more refined interface and better functionality. For example, Teleplace Multi-Share's fine-grained collaboration technology allows multiple users to see how others are editing or modifying content in real time. Teleplace includes webcam video conferencing, so you can use it to hold traditional video conferences. All communications between users are automatically encrypted, ensuring security of information.

Even more important, Teleplace Multi-Share is built upon the open source Croquet platform. From Croquet, Teleplace inherited the use of open standards—the Python programming language for scripting and standard XML interfaces for application integration. Both of these are common in the software developer community, making it easy to find a qualified software professional to customize or amend the platform for a specific application (although a list of developers is nowhere to be found on the Teleplace website). In a corporate environment, Teleplace Multi-Share would work best for facilitating remote business meetings. In other areas, such as training or 3-D visualization, it might be limited by the lack of building and scripting tools as well as lack of an application program-

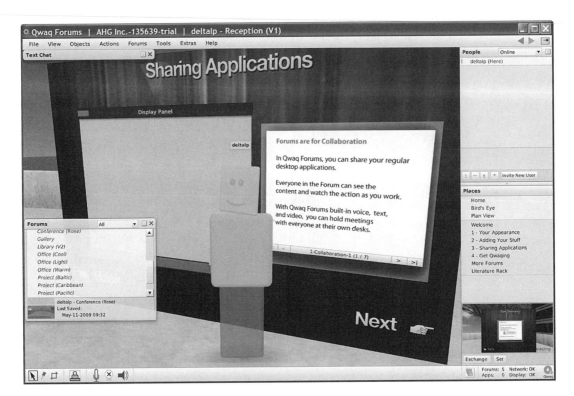

FIGURE 3.5

ming interface (API) that would allow third-party developers to "extend" the base software.

Teleplace operates out of a Redwood City, California, location and lists Intel and British Petroleum among its customers (Teleplace 2009).

Second Life (www.secondlife.com, www.secondlifegrid.com)

Second Life is the one of the most mature (it opened to the public in June of 2003) and perhaps the best known of the virtual worlds we review here (Figure 3.6). If we had to pinpoint a single reason for that, we would quote a *PC Magazine* review written only a few months after the official open-

FIGURE 3.6

ing of Second Life: "Of all the virtual worlds we visited, Second Life is the one we want to come back to the most" (Costa 2003). We attribute this to the fact that Linden Lab—the company behind Second Life—has created a virtual world that comes with easy-to-use 3-D modeling software in which you can reproduce those aspects of the physical world that *you* find interesting and want to use for your specific purposes.

Ease of use was of critical importance for Linden Lab in designing Second Life (Figure 3.7). The ability to instantly—and without a significant investment required by other sophisticated virtual worlds—become a creator, an architect, a manufacturer, and a merchant quickly attracted a core group of innovative early adopters who did not necessarily have a technical background. They started to use the platform for informal social interaction. Natural evolution, user feedback, and the attraction of more technical people facilitated the development of sophisticated tools, which, in turn, attracted an entirely new generation of users. Training specialists, educators, marketing executives, and businesspeople who were initially intrigued by the social scene of Second Life quickly recognized the potential of the platform for their professional activities.

You can readily preview the capabilities of the platform by opening a free account. With the free account you receive access to an extensive set of tools: a library of objects, textures, and sounds; a physics engine; the ability to communicate using text, note cards, and voice; basic social networking tools (the ability to search for other users and to form groups); the ability to script objects' behaviors; and a working economy, with Linden dollars fully convertible into real currency. This "starter package" is undoubtedly the largest and the most functional of all the virtual world offerings. To obtain anything of this magnitude in competing virtual worlds, you would need to spend tens of thousands of dollars and/or significant time doing your own building and programming. By realizing cost avoidance from the start, you can immediately concentrate on your business objectives.

Many of the tools that you do not receive as a part of the initial package (for example, business-type clothes for your avatar, a screen capable

FIGURE 3.7

of showing slides or streaming video, a quiz tool that can be connected to your LMS or database, or even a simulation testing how well a group of people would work as a team) you will find free or for a very reasonable fee from independent "in-world" vendors (people doing business and/or advertising their wares within Second Life). Other tools and objects that you might want or need can be obtained from third-party vendors specializing in these services.

Because Second Life is the most populous virtual world, you will find contractors specializing in all aspects of business—from helping you to organize and build a secure corporate campus to managing large events to automating your training program with custom robotic avatars that can play almost any role that you want. Linden Lab provides open access to a database of qualified developers in your country and around the world (http://secondlife.com/solution_providers/listings .php). As of this writing, the database contained 230 Second Life developers and consultants, 123 of them in the United States.

One of the reasons for the popularity of Second Life is an ease with which you can try it and a clear path of program development. After creating a free account on the website, you download the Second Life client and log into the virtual world. The first time you log in, you find yourself on one of the "orientation islands" where you go through a boot camp, learning how to do basic things: walk, fly, sit, and touch an object.

Organizations can create a custom login process that allows employees to log into a specified location on the company's island and go through a customized onboarding process. If you decide that a Second Life project is worth pursuing, you need to purchase your own virtual land so that you—or developers you contract—will be able to start building, scripting, and creating your content, be it collaboration space or training simulations. You can set up security parameters allowing or disallowing free access to the whole island or its specific areas.

From a technical standpoint, a virtual island is simply a dedicated server located in the Linden Lab's network operations center. Since the company was founded in 1999, it has been consistently expanding its operations and increasing their reliability. Today Linden Lab has a distributed network of offices with more than 250 employees in the United States, Europe, and Asia. The central office is located in San Francisco, California. Linden Lab has academia, government, and corporate customers in most industries spanning the alphabet from Advertising to Wireless Communications.

Conclusions

Out of the group of five virtual worlds that satisfy all or most of the criteria for business use, three—Forterra's OLIVE, ProtonMedia's Protosphere, and OpenSim—can be installed on a corporate network. Two others—Teleplace and Second Life—selected the "software as a service" (SaaS) model. They operate data centers running multiple servers—that is, virtual land—and users access these servers using custom software (clients) provided by respective vendors. This seems to be a concern for some of the corporate users who prefer to keep everything inside their own network. In March of 2008, Linden Lab and IBM teamed up to build enterprise-ready virtual worlds that can be deployed behind a customer's firewall (Brodkin 2008), and in July of the same year they reached a high level of interoperability (Second Life Blog 2008). A few months later Linden Lab started an independent project on building a stand-alone, behind-the-firewall version of Second Life. As of this writing (May 2009), this project has completed an alpha test stage that seems to have been very successful. By the time you read this book, an option for corporate customers to purchase a private version of Second Life and install it on their network should be available. This hindrance out of the way, we think that at the present time, Second Life beats the competition for most projects.

Second Life offers multilevel high-granularity access control allowing you to assign access privileges based on various parameters such as location or group assignment. Today the platform has high-quality customizable avatars and landscape elements, and Linden Lab continues to enhance the visual components of a user's 3-D experience. A graphical user interface (GUI) allows even beginners to experiment with the way their avatars and their virtual environments look and behave. Multimodal communication tools allow easy collaboration, and addition of encrypted text and voice are on the company's "to do" list.

From a security standpoint, it is important that Second Life projects can be connected to and exchange data with an outside database or learning management system. As a result, even if you select to host your virtual island on Linden Lab's network, you can keep proprietary data in a database located on *your* network, protected by *your* corporate firewall, and retrieve it on an as-needed basis. Add to this the availability of secure encryption and you will keep your Second Life project and associated data as safe as when using other Internet applications.

Recent versions of the Second Life client include the ability to import 3-D graphics from other programs, such as 3D Studio and Blender. No doubt these capabilities will continue to expand, helping you use existing materials in your virtual world project.

You also cannot disregard the value of a small upfront investment. Unlike most of the competition, Second Life fees are transparent and can be easily found on the website (as of May 2009, the price for a virtual island was a $1,000 setup fee, plus $295 per month). Even with added developer and/or consulting costs, the total upfront investment can be as little as one-fifth to one-tenth of the start-up fees of competing virtual worlds. This allows you to start with a small pilot project and gradually expand, adjusting the project specifications based on your own results.

Lack of reliability used to be a major impediment for the serious use of Second Life. To a large degree, this resulted from the explosive growth that Linden Lab experienced in the first five years of Second Life's existence. In 2008 the company invested heavily in both hardware and seasoned network professionals, cutting outages in half. Owners of virtual land (but not regular users) have access to 24/7 phone support.

Real life independently validates Second Life's advantage over the competition. The number of corporations running successful projects in Second Life by far exceeds the alternative solutions and grows continuously, as demonstrated by the case studies in the chapters that follow.

Linden Lab and Second Life in Their Own Words: Enterprise-Related Developments and Future Plans

Second Life, intentionally or not, stealthily grew into a major player in the enterprise virtual world sector, a market segment that includes business, education, nonprofit, and government customers. Early corporate adopters have already increased effectiveness and quality of training, collaboration, HR, professional certification, and compliance by using Second Life, while Linden Lab continues active development of the platform, adapting it to enterprise requirements.

> " I never worry about action, but only inaction."
> —*Winston Churchill*

Enterprise and Consumer Segments

Although Second Life started as a pure consumer play, by late 2008 Linden Lab was receiving roughly 20 percent of revenue from the enterprise market. According to Mark Kingdon, CEO of Linden Lab, the company sees its enterprise offerings in the context of the platform strategy. In plain English, this means that as a platform, Second Life must accommodate a wide variety of use cases in a meaningful way. At the same time, the management team sees Second Life as a mature product that requires and benefits from being tailored to specific market segments.

In late 2008, Linden Lab created a product development master plan for all market segments, identifying a road map of improvements in both the consumer and enterprise sectors. A couple of things worth mentioning in the consumer sector are

- ▶ simplifying the "first-hour experience"
- ▶ recent acquisitions of e-commerce companies

A newly minted user's first-hour experience of creating a new account, logging into Second Life for the first time, and getting acquainted with the virtual world is, perhaps, the most complex and potentially frustrating period of a user's virtual world life. The fact that Linden Lab put the tasks of simplification and making the first-hour experience more inviting at the top of its list is very promising. And, acquisitions in the area of Web-based e-commerce complement Linden Lab's in-world commerce platform.

More interesting for us is the decision by Linden Lab to focus its management team on increasing capabilities and power on the enterprise side of the platform. There are two major developments here:

1. Fine-tuning of the technology to accommodate the needs of an enterprise: (a) creating "behind-the-firewall" virtual world solutions, (b) creating virtual world standards and working on interoperability among virtual worlds, (c) expanding the independent third-party developer base that is oriented toward corporate customer and working with the developers, (d) adding business tools such as text and voice encryption and media/application sharing
2. Customer education—perfecting the company's message and value-based proposition for both hosted and "behind-the-firewall" solutions to educate and attract corporate customers

Enterprise Technology

Many enterprise customers told Linden Lab that they wanted a "behind-the-firewall" solution. That is, they want to have all the benefits of Second Life in a "private world" that they can host on their corporate network. Creating this type of environment will give an enterprise a greater sense of comfort and security. It will also bring on board companies that simply cannot use hosted solutions (defense contractors, for example). Since stand-alone virtual worlds will service only corporate network customers and will not tie into the main grid (that is, other servers hosting Second Life virtual worlds), they will allow customers even more flexibility in setting privacy, security, and access parameters.

In early 2009, Linden Lab completed the alpha testing part of this project with a small group of enterprise customers and—after reviewing results, fixing bugs, and making modifications—will go into beta testing in the second half of 2009.

Another high-priority technical aspect on the map is interoperability—the ability of a user to reach different virtual worlds using one interface, or one client. This is fairly similar to using one Web browser to view all kinds of Internet and intranet websites.

Interoperability became the focus of a recent joint Linden Lab and IBM project. The pilot project (completed in 2008) was "designed to allow IBM employees to explore the Second Life mainland and seamlessly cross over into IBM's custom-built world behind the firewall without having to log on and off. . . . The goal [was] to allow IBM employees to access public spaces and private spaces within one Second Life client interface while privatizing and securing portions of the Second Life Grid behind IBM's firewall" (IBM 2008). Eventually, solutions similar to this pilot project will become available to all enterprise customers.

Hosted Solution

A hosted solution, or having your virtual world hosted by Linden Lab in one of its network operations centers, maintains its own appeal. The upfront investment is significantly lower, and you do not need to involve an IT department in maintaining new hardware and software. A hosted solution may satisfy the needs of some, perhaps many, enterprise customers, while for others it can work as a fast and cheap "proof of concept" way to try Second Life training and communication capabilities. Any content created in hosted Second Life will run on a stand-alone version and vice versa.

Linden Lab plans to add several new business-related features to both behind-the-firewall and hosted solutions. Among them are text (chat, instant messages) and voice encryption and media/application sharing. Since 2008, Second Life users can create customized entry paths—a custom registration process that leads to a specific, tailored-to-your-needs orientation session. You can also create a restricted avatar name so that all employees of your organization, and only they, will have the same last name—your company name, for example, making it easy to immediately distinguish between an employee and a visitor. This proved to be an important feature for corporations, so now Linden Lab is creating a separate entry path tailored to business customers. On a personal level, this makes Second Life more inviting, intuitively familiar, and appealing to a corporate user.

Simultaneously the company changed its land-use strategy to accommodate corporate needs. Similar to the physical world, where a business address is important and businesses tend to group in clusters reflecting their synergies, in-world "proximity" and "zoning" are becoming meaningful concepts.

Customer Education

Second Life is perhaps the most versatile virtual world platform with the easiest point of entry and lowest ongoing costs. However, until recently Linden Lab failed to communicate its value proposition to enterprise customers, especially in communicating the benefits of a hosted solution. Often this failure was exacerbated by media's obsession with certain parts of the consumer sector. Perhaps Linden Lab needs to do a fair amount of education of enterprise buyers to explain that the platform, even as it exists today, addresses a number of security and privacy concerns that companies might have. Along with working on dependability, scalability, security, privacy, and technical requirements of the corporate world, Linden Lab increased the head count of its enterprise team. It hired both technical and marketing professionals to organize seminars and to provide bidirectional communication channels for both "behind-the-firewall" and hosted solutions.

As of this writing, Second Life averages eighty-five thousand concurrent users at any given moment. Linden Lab expects this number to grow to a hundred thousand by the end of 2009, with a significant part of the increase due to enterprise customers. The way things are going, we will not be surprised if the company exceeds its own projections.

Deploying a Corporate Training Program in Second Life

finally, after discussing who, what, and where, perhaps we have whetted your appetite enough to start discussing the real thing—your first training program in a virtual world. Starting a successful training program does not depend on the medium, and since it is likely to be a team effort, there are a few questions you might want to discuss with your team.

> "There are two mistakes one can make along the road to truth . . . not going all the way, and not starting."
> —*Hindu Prince Gautama Siddharta, the founder of Buddhism, 563–483 B.C.*

Defining the Goal

Show us a failed project—any project, not necessarily related to virtual worlds—and we will show you poorly defined goals. What areas of your corporate training will benefit from expansion into a virtual world? What do you want to see as an outcome? The answers depend on the industry; corporate culture; budget; and age, background, and education of the workforce as much as they depend on the nature of the medium you select for training and other corporate uses.

Start with the basics: What outcome would add most to the company's bottom line? What aspect of your current training is the most expensive and takes the longest time? Or even better: do you have a training area that is failing? Michelin came to virtual worlds *not* because it set its sights on becoming the first multinational corporation to start a training program in Second Life. It decided to start a Second Life training program because every other training method it tried failed. Michelin's enterprise architecture approach is renowned for its complexity. Prior to Second Life training, employees complained of having to deal with too many concepts. They did not see the material's relevance to their everyday work and thought it was too difficult to understand.

Objective metrics confirmed that all the types of training Michelin tried were not working. Using Second Life as a training platform changed all that. In order to get there, Michelin first set two very specific and very simple goals for training in Second Life: (1) to create an environment for a small team of people studying under the supervision of an instructor, and (2) to create a place for individual trainees to come back to on a regular basis for practice after attending the course. The immersive nature of Second Life allowed trainees to practice scenarios for one of the real-life situations and eventually to learn and use complex concepts (see Michelin case study on using Second Life, Chapter 7).

Do you spend money and effort on recruiting? Do you want to select self-learners whose curiosity is stimulated by a demanding task? TMP Worldwide set the goal of using Second Life in a recruiting effort for its clients. The aim was to help it to break out of the clutter and stand out in communicating its brand as an employer of choice (see TMP Worldwide case study, Chapter 11). EMC Corporation saw Second Life's benefit in both branding the company as *the* place to work and as an opportunity to reach hidden talent in noncommon locations, while avoiding the expense of travel and attracting sophisticated candidates (see EMC case study, Chapter 11). Selected goals led to a specific plan of action that was successfully implemented.

Would your company benefit from stronger collaboration, especially if you have geographically dispersed teams? Would it benefit from a 3-D environment? Would you benefit from multimodal communications? The experiences of Microsoft and Intel show that if your goals include building a team consisting of physically disconnected people, Second Life might be your tool of choice (see Microsoft and Intel case studies, Chapter 6).

An effective training program starts with a clear outline of the desired results. Learning goals can be described from the perspective of cognition (what knowledge must be transferred to the trainees), actions (procedures that trainees need to learn, memorizing what should be done and in what order), and emotions (how trainees should react to the known real-life situations, i.e., what are known emotional pitfalls). Training programs to fulfill each of these goals might include facts, concepts, principles, and procedures, delivered in such a way that trainees will make tacit "theoretical knowledge" their own explicit "actionable knowledge." Note that none of these goals depends on parameters such as "coolness" or the ability to use the latest media-hyped tools that sometimes are cited as the reason to create a virtual world training program.

 ## What Works and What Does Not in the New Medium

According to the philosopher Gilbert Ryle (1949) there are two main types of knowledge: "knowing that" (also called descriptive, declarative, or explicit knowledge) and "knowing how" (also called procedural, experiential, or tacit knowledge) (see also Polanyi 1966, Borgmann 1999).

Descriptive knowledge can be explained, interpreted, and discussed. This distinguishes it from experiential knowledge—hands-on "know-how" of a specific task such as riding a bicycle, making an effective sales presentation in front of a large audience, or operating a piece of equipment. "Of the three ways in which men think that they acquire knowledge of things—authority, reasoning, and experience—only the last is effective and able to bring peace to the intellect," wrote Roger Bacon in the thirteenth century. Yet, until recently, it was thought that the only way to transfer experiential knowledge effectively was face-to-face training. By its very nature, experiential knowledge—be it machinery operation or sales training specific to a company's product—is the most difficult and expensive to transfer within an organization. Prior to the emergence of the virtual worlds it was especially challenging within the context of distance or computer-based training. Reading, or watching video or slides—typical methods of acquiring descriptive knowledge—work poorly, if at all.

Procedural knowledge, skills that require practice and experience, on the other hand, finds a great medium in virtual worlds. Preparing a patient for surgery, for example, is a very complex *procedure* that involves multiple steps with numerous decision points branching into additional subprocedures. Traditional training is extremely time- and effort-consuming and involves the use of real operating rooms and equipment. Teaching future nurses the procedure of preparing a patient for surgery in Second Life (see University of Kansas Medical Center case study, Chapter 10) has proved to be very successful. In general, training that requires learners to perform an operating process or procedure (especially within a complex decision tree), or requires 3-D visualization, will gain from being conducted in a virtual world.

Interactivity is another built-in feature you need to consider when thinking about using Second Life or other virtual worlds. Probably all of us have witnessed instructors lecturing on teamwork or leadership to a group of people sitting in an auditorium. Regardless of the quality of such a lecture, it is as productive as teaching swimming without water. In virtual worlds, this type of subject is taught using interactive simulations. Examples include people working together on an obstacle course, trying to solve a puzzle, or completing any project that requires teamwork.

Since data on the actions of each team member can be recorded, Second Life even has an advantage over real-life teamwork and leadership training. The instructor has lots of data on the performance of each team member and, therefore, a good foundation for discussing results, drawing conclusions, and planning for future training. Given that teams can do something "not serious" (e.g., "just playing with a puzzle"), team members usually feel more secure and less defensive and are more open to a frank dialogue on their personal and team actions. Thus, teamwork training really becomes training as opposed to listening to another lecture.

Another type of activity that has gained a lot of traction in virtual worlds is collaboration. From the experience of companies such as Intel, Microsoft, and many others, we know that about the only situation in which meetings, lectures, seminars, presentations, and other typical descriptive knowledge projects work is when they trigger two-way communication and collaboration. Using Second Life for meetings or lectures often seems to be a logical place to test virtual worlds as a platform with a usual "baby steps" approach. Saving time and resources on travel certainly does not hurt as well.

Simply moving meetings or classes into a virtual world, however, will often leave participants wondering, why were they asked to use new technology? What could not be done using any of the more familiar methods? Did they really need to do it?

Even the most intellectually curious among us are generally conservative in how we go about our everyday business. If participants do not see an immediate overwhelming benefit of using a new technology, rejecting it is only a natural instinct. A lukewarm reception "in the trenches" might curtail the project even before the team has had a chance to test and appreciate the strongest aspects of virtual worlds—on-demand procedural training and interactive assessments, along with more apparent collaboration and communication applications. Avoid this pitfall by using virtual worlds for brainstorming and discussions. Encourage multimodal communications—simultaneous use of voice, text, and instant messages. Take advantage of graphical tools such as mind mapping software. Visualize project elements, such as time lines, deliverables, vendors, and their relationship within the project.

The other side of successful interactive applications of virtual worlds is the failure of static installations. If your project's goal is to attract external visitors for marketing or recruiting, for example, you need to make sure that they have something to do besides wandering in an empty, lifeless space. Nothing kills externally oriented projects faster and more reliably than a well-built virtual world copy of a corporate campus, idly sitting on an empty island without any activity going on. At the same time, internal use areas for training or collaboration do not require as much attention in terms of filling the void when they are not in use. Just make sure that private-access internal use areas are clearly separated from the public-access externally oriented sections.

Starting small and gradually introducing new aspects of a technology is a good idea. However, do not mistake starting small with the path of least resistance. Beginning with seemingly comfortable pieces while leaving out perhaps less familiar but more valuable aspects will often diminish the value of the project.

What Is a Second Life Island?

Just as in the physical world or on the Internet, the first thing you need for a project in Second Life is a location—a piece of real estate. From a technical standpoint, virtual worlds are almost identical to the Web except for different terminology. Whereas websites are hosted on servers, in the case of Second Life it is common to talk about "private regions," "islands," or "simulators." These words are synonymous. An island in Second Life is an analog of a Web server. It is a dedicated computer processor running special software. This software creates a location in a virtual world. You see this location as a piece of land 256 meters by 256 meters in size. It has the ability to support fifteen thousand primitives, or "prims"—the building blocks from which everything in Second Life is made—and up to one hundred users simultaneously. If you have purchased real estate in Second Life, you can control your private region. Specifically, you can authorize or limit access to the island; set the number of people allowed to visit the island simultaneously; create variable user groups with different access privileges; change everything about the island's appearance, including terrain and landscape; create separate areas with their own access control; control sound and streaming media; create objects; and run scripts.

A private region can be viewed as a part of an "estate"—a collection of one or more private regions managed together under one set of rules. If the estate includes more than one region, these regions do *not* have to be contiguous, although they can be. Estates can have only one designated owner, but they can be paid for by more than one person or company.

A network of Second Life private regions creates a "grid" that allows a user to travel from one island to another, similar to visiting different websites. As of this writing, there are two Second Life grids: one for a general audience and one for teens only.

As we have previously noted, Linden Lab is working on software that will allow companies to install servers running Second Life on their own corporate networks. Once it becomes available—and chances are, it will be available by the time you read this book—corporate customers will be able to build its own grids in a protected environment on their corporate networks. Until then you have two choices: purchase a server hosted by Linden Lab on its grid or, if you want to start really small, lease a part of an island owned by someone else. The first choice gives you more freedom in what you can do in terms of building and programming, and it allows you to set up your own security and privacy options. With the latter you will save some money but will have less control, as well as fewer prims available for building and a reduced number of concurrent users. You will also depend on your "landlord" to allow scripting, landscape your area, and provide security. If the landlord cuts back on virtual world presence, sells the island to a new owner, or makes other changes, you run the risk of losing some or all of your work.

Current prices for owning a Second Life island are quite reasonable. An initial fee of $1,000 and a monthly maintenance fee of $295 make you the owner of a private region. There are two other options targeted toward light use: Homestead Private Region and Openspace Private Region, but realistically they cannot support any kind of corporate use due to severe limitations on the number of available prims (3,750 and 750, respectively) and concurrent users (twenty and ten, respectively).

 ## Building Environment and Instructional Design Considerations

Once you own real estate, it is time to start creating content. There are several points you need to consider and discuss with your team before you give directions to your chief builder. The general design of a corporate area often becomes an initial point of contention. The first idea that often comes to mind is "let's build a copy of our office in the virtual world." We recommend that you fight this idea, expel it from your mind, and never admit you ever thought of doing something like that! Building a copy of real buildings in a virtual world is almost never a good idea. Reasons for this are easy to understand:

> ▶ It never rains or snows in Second Life. Elements will not interfere with your project, so there is little benefit to having a roof over your head. Actually, for added security you can build a literal roof over parts of or all of your private region. It will protect your island from being automatically mapped—or, rather, the map will show one big roof. The roof, however, does not need to rest on walls, columns, or other support structures. If you really need a roof for security reasons, you can simply hang it in the air a couple hundred meters above the land. Sometimes you might want to have meetings and conversations in a secure environment and you cannot limit access to the whole island—if this is the case, walls and a roof over a controlled-access perimeter are beneficial. However, try to keep paths wide for easy access, and either limit the building to one story or use "elevator" scripts that will allow people to travel between floors without the necessity of negotiating stairways.

▶ Employees do not need an office in Second Life. They are there to collaborate with their peers and to work with their colleagues or customers, not to sit behind a virtual desk.

▶ For beginners, walking down a narrow hall in a virtual world without hitting a wall is an exercise they do not need.

▶ People will not move to the virtual world for eight working hours per day; they will continue to work at their regular locations, so the corporate campus will be empty most of the time. You will find better use of your budget.

Of course, you do need to think through and equip work locations in Second Life. To do this, you can split the land into several parcels. Each parcel can have its own access and privilege rules, so that different groups of employees can have access to different parcels and the ability (or inability) to perform specific tasks at these locations.

Each of the parcels can be dedicated to a particular project and equipped correspondingly. For example, if you plan to have a place for collaboration and meetings of a geographically dispersed team, it makes sense to equip the parcel with collaboration tools: a screen to show slides, a whiteboard, and a mind-mapping tool for brainstorming sessions. If another parcel is used to train salespeople, you can use it to build a model of the office similar to that of one of your clients. There the salespeople will actually work and use it for the immersive training. In fact, building a model of a real-life environment is warranted only when it is a part of training. For example, you might need a model of an operating room to train nurses or a model of a factory floor to train personnel in emergency procedures. Building a copy of your corporate headquarters to show off will do little even in the way of showing off. And, please, avoid clutter.

Second Life has great tools that allow you to keep an object or a set of objects in what is called "inventory." This is similar to keeping a document as a file on the hard drive of your computer (Figure 5.1). When you need to work with a file, you open it. Similarly, when you need an object, you "pull"

FIGURE 5.1

it out from your inventory. You do not keep all your files open on your screen all at the same time. Similarly, keeping your virtual world organized pays by making your Second Life work immensely more productive.

Making Virtual Worlds Interactive: Basic Scripting

To make a Second Life environment interactive, or to build training tools and simulations in Second Life, you need objects that behave in a certain manner and react to the user's actions. This is accomplished by scripting. Scripts are written in a special Linden Scripting Language, which resembles other scripting languages such as JavaScript. The language is event-driven, meaning it allows a programmer to respond to events that happen with and around an object (for example, someone clicks on it, touches it, collides with it, moves it, appears near it, etc.). There are a number of built-in functions that allow an item to respond to an event, but scripting will require the skills of a programmer. At this time there are no recognized qualifications in Second Life scripting, so when selecting a contractor for your project you will need to rely exclusively on the demonstrated experience.

Are They Ready? A Case for Instructional Design

Virtual worlds, just as any other technology, require careful consideration in terms of workforce preparedness. If people who are supposed to receive training are not comfortable using new technology, that technology will never become a positive force in the corporate world.

Ask yourself, "Who is the target audience?" Projects targeting technical personnel, sales, management, new hires, and different generational and educational groups will require different degrees of pretraining and learning. This means that the design of your virtual world environment should correspond not only to the activity that you are planning but also to the audience that will use it.

Second Life has plenty of tools allowing creation of easy-to-navigate spaces that will make an orientation session short and productive. For example, a nontechnical audience might have problems logging into Second Life for the first time and reaching/walking to a specific destination. When working with this type of user, you are well advised to pre-create their avatars and build a system that will automatically log their avatars into the correct location. If you design plenty of interactive directory signs (Figure 5.2), a simple click on a button could transfer the person to the exact location, and you will not frustrate new users with learning how to navigate in a virtual world. They will learn how to walk and fly in Second Life nevertheless, but will do it gradually, without even paying attention to the fact that they are learning something new and unusual. In the meantime, people will be free to devote their time to the task at hand, be it training, communicating, or other tasks.

With a workforce less experienced in modern computing, we recommend one or two hours of live introductory sessions with instructors ready to help learners through their first steps in a virtual world. In our experience, if people feel overwhelmed by their first experience in Second Life, the problem lies with the instructional design. You bring employees into Second Life so that they will learn something new about their work and about business, and have a better opportunity to collaborate with colleagues, *not* to learn how to fly in Second Life, how to change the look of their avatar, or how to find fancy clothes. A good practice is to determine specific skills that employees will need to perform their tasks in Second Life and teach only those skills. For example, the University of Kansas Medical Center limited general Second Life instruction to ten minutes, and that was enough to teach students the basics of moving, focusing, and interacting with the objects. Michelin devoted significantly more time to the introduction to Second Life but, by its own account, found that most of it was unnecessary.

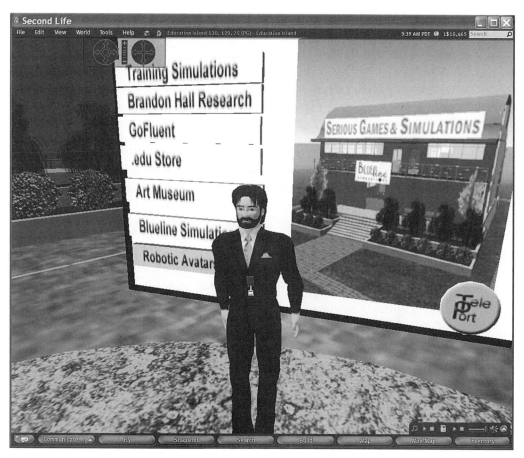

FIGURE 5.2

Synchronous vs. Asynchronous Training

Until recently, corporate acceptance of Second Life as a platform for training, recruiting, marketing, and other business activities was hindered by the assumption that these activities have to be conducted only in real time. Instructors must be present along with the learners at the same time and lead the training.

In the past, recruiting or new-hire orientation was conducted by company representatives who were present and leading the project at all times in what we call the synchronous mode. E-learning developments of the past ten to fifteen years have taught us the value of asynchronous training, where trainees are able to learn and practice on their own at any time of the day. An instructor serves as a figure of authority and a safety net and is not necessarily present during most of the training or new-hire orientation. While early attempts at conducting training in Second Life have been, for the most part, in synchronous mode, two recent developments have changed the situation.

The first of these developments is the ability to connect a training simulation in Second Life to a database outside the Second Life network. This database can be connected to, or be a part of, your learning management system (LMS). LMSs generally use database software to store required information about classes, training sessions, employees, grades, schedules, certifications, and other relevant data. Most of the learning management systems also give you access to what software engineers call an application programming interface (API)—a set of programs and rules that allow computer programmers to interconnect two or more different pieces of software.

Having facilities to connect Second Life simulations to a database, along with access to a learning management system's APIs, allows programmers to connect Second Life simulation to your LMS. As a result, training professionals receive full access to administrating and delivering Second Life training as well as accessing results through a familiar LMS interface. If you do not use an LMS, or you do not want to connect Second Life simulations to your LMS, you can connect a simulation to a standalone database. You can use this database strictly to keep and manage data necessary for Second Life simulations.

In both cases, Second Life simulation can be added as another module to your e-learning program. Learners can log into Second Life and complete assigned simulation(s) at any time. Results of their activities will be recorded in an LMS or stand-alone database, and instructors will have enough information to draw conclusions about learners' skills and knowledge to see if further training is warranted. Second Life programs communicate through the same computer port as all websites (normally, port 80, or, if you prefer to use secure encrypted connection, port 443). Therefore, an information technology department does not need to change anything in the firewall or network settings to allow exchange of information between a Second Life simulation and your internal database or LMS. This significantly simplifies and expedites implementation of Second Life training.

Connecting Second Life simulations to an outside database allows you to keep all the information, including sensitive and intellectual property data, outside Second Life, on your enterprise network behind the firewall, making project implementation more secure.

Another interesting recent development that brings Second Life into the realm of everyday, asynchronous e-learning is the introduction of robotic avatars, or virtual agents. Robotic avatars look and act as if they represent real people, but in fact they are operated by computer software. Robotic avatars are indispensable in tasks that require interactivity, such as sales training, dealing with difficult people, new-hire orientation, and demonstrating the use of equipment. Along with teaching the assigned task, the system logs the interaction with robotic avatars for future assessment by a trainee and an instructor. Robotic avatar software and training-related data are located on a corporate network outside Second Life; therefore, data security is drastically improved.

Security Considerations

Since we mentioned security, let us talk about it in more detail. Potential users have several concerns when they think about using Second Life in a corporate environment. These concerns can be separated into two groups: features that can be modified and features that cannot be modified using regular Second Life controls. The first group generally includes:

▶ The ability to limit access to the island as a whole or to certain parts of the island to a specific group of people

▶ The ability to limit access to all data or parts of data and intellectual property to a specific person or a group of people

▶ The ability to limit access to simulations, or even to look at available simulations and their qualities, and execution of scripts; the power to limit ability to modify items to a specific person or a group of people

▶ The ability to carry on private conversations by text or by voice

The second group includes concerns about corporate data security. The location of a Second Life server on the outside network requires reconfiguring settings or opening additional ports in order to use Second Life from your enterprise network. We review both groups of security concerns and the ways to address them here.

Modifiable Security Settings

Islands, or Second Life private regions, provide a set of tools that allow an owner to control access to the island or a specific parcel of land by creating access lists. Individuals not on the list will not be able to access protected areas. Similarly, you can create a list of individuals specifically banned from an island or a specific parcel.

The ability to run scripts and move or modify objects is also controlled through a Second Life graphical user interface and can be accomplished easily.

An island is surrounded by a significant void space, represented by water. It cannot be crossed by walking, running, flying, or using camera controls. Outside users, if not allowed onto your island, can generally view the conceptual contents of the island; outlines of buildings, for example, appear as if viewed from extreme altitude on a "world map." However, as we mentioned, constructing a high, impermeable "roof" above your private region will make structures and objects in the private region invisible to outside users.

A private region is generally secure from eavesdropping. There is, however, a security concern even on properly secured private regions. An attacker can create a seemingly innocuous object, such as a piece of furniture, an art object, a wristwatch, or a piece of clothing, containing a script that makes this object record conversations and/or local avatar and object names. Once brought into a secure area or given to an unsuspecting employee, such an object could record and transmit private data.

It is relatively easy to prevent and defend against such attacks. First, all employees should be aware of a company policy not to bring any outside items into a secure area. Violation of such policy should be considered a serious lapse. Second, the Second Life viewer allows an administrator to view a list of all scripts that are running in the private regions, sorted by the computing resources they consume. A "listener" spy device would be on top of such a list, since it uses a lot of computing power, so it can be easily located and deleted. It is generally a good practice to monitor the list of running scripts and investigate anything suspicious.

More good news: a script cannot listen to instant messages, including group instant messages (unless the instant message is sent specifically to the scripted object), voice communications, or media streams. Scripts also cannot directly capture visual content, such as objects or textures.

Streaming video and audio travel directly from the server that streams the data to your Second Life client. They *do not* pass through Second Life servers; therefore, the security of voice/audio and video data is the same as the security of similar data when using Web conferencing or voice over IP (VoIP) tools. When streaming audio or video content, you can use the secure Web protocol (you can recognize it by the letter *s* at the end of the protocol name in the Web address—*https://*) for enhanced security.

Voice data pass through the servers owned by Vivox, the company that provides Second Life's voice communication technology. You can set up how you want to hear voice communications: from the position of your avatar (you will hear voice for up to sixty meters from your avatar's position) or from the position of the camera (up to fifty meters from camera position). As a result, your hearing cannot traverse a void space to "listen in" on conversations taking place in the other private regions. Even if your avatar is invisible to those around you, your avatar name always appears in the "Near Me" list of voice listeners and speakers.

Linden Lab plans to offer encrypted voice communications in the near future. Until that time, if you are concerned about unencrypted voice communications, you can either disable voice or use an alternative voice channel that provides encryption, such as the ubiquitous Skype (www .skype.com).

Data Security in Second Life

Linden Lab seems to understand the importance of data security to its customers. Servers running Second Life reside in secure hosted facilities. Your private region runs on servers hosted specifically for Linden Lab, as do all backbone data services, including inventory, server logs, communication, and other content. Physical access to the network operation center is limited to a "need to perform work" basis. As a private region owner, if you are concerned about Linden Lab's employee activity, you may ask it to verify its activity and it will respond promptly.

To prevent remote attacks, servers do not "trust" the client (Second Life viewer). Access requires a login token to establish your identity and permissions, including land access. The privilege verification system makes it practically impossible to impersonate other clients or accounts. Multiple concurrent logins for the same account are disallowed, so if you leave your computer logged in and try to log into Second Life from a different computer, the first session will be discontinued.

Second Life maintains several types of servers. "Land servers" keep data on land and combined data on objects and avatars. Content, that is all objects and scripts that you create in Second Life, is stored separately from the land servers on so-called asset servers. Every hour, Linden Lab automatically runs backup procedure, so if something goes wrong you can restore the contents for a time point no further back than an hour. These backups are retained with decreasing frequency as they age.

In April 2008, Linden Lab announced a future capability for IBM to host simulators behind its firewall. Hosting by IBM will provide some alternate security features compared to standard hosting by Linden Lab, due to some changes to the configuration of the simulator. In July 2008, IBM and Linden Lab announced that their research teams had teleported avatars from the Second Life preview grid into a virtual world running on an OpenSim server. This is widely seen as an important step toward interoperability between Second Life and other virtual worlds.

Perhaps even more important, for corporate use of Second Life, this is also a move toward greater security. Region content *and* inventory, as well as chat logs for the IBM-hosted regions, reside on IBM's servers. Linden Lab's employees may be disallowed access to that content. In this manner, you can secure all assets and chat logs for your private regions. Your environment becomes accessible only to employees who have access to your hosted servers and to those on the Second Life grid to whom you have specifically granted access.

Simultaneously, Linden Lab is putting a lot of effort into developing a project, code-named "Nebraska," that will allow a customer to keep a Second Life server on its network, behind its own firewall. Since other parameters are going to be similar to those of the joint Linden Lab/IBM project—ability to keep content, inventory, and chat logs on your own server—this promises to be a very positive development.

Currently (May 2009) Linden Lab is conducting an alpha test of stand-alone Second Life servers at organizations such as IBM, Naval Undersea Warfare Center (NUWC), New Media Consortium (NMC), Intel, and Northrop Grumman. The company plans to go into a beta phase in the summer of 2009, so by the time this book is published, the results of the beta test should be available to the public. It might be possible that a commercial version of Nebraska will be available at that time as well.

To summarize, by the time this book is published, there are likely to be three ways to establish a presence in Second Life. The first one (the traditional way) is available as of this writing.

1. **Traditional way.** Keep your private region co-located (occupying a part of the server) on Linden Lab's network. Simulations and data can still be located on any server outside Linden Lab's network—for example, on your corporate network behind your firewall.
2. **IBM server.** Keep your private region co-located on IBM's network. Regional content, inventory, and chat logs will reside on IBM's servers, and Linden Lab's personnel will not have access to this data.
3. **Private co-location.** Keep your private region on your corporate network. Only your personnel will have access to all settings and all data.

All three hosting options are technically compatible. If you start with a traditional hosting on the Linden Lab network, you can later move your content to a private server on your network and vice versa.

New Worlds, New Tools

As you start working with virtual worlds, you will probably discover that creating objects, an environment, and simulations in virtual worlds for employee training, as well as collaboration and other corporate purposes, sometimes requires more specialized tools than those that come as a part of the software platform. Fortunately, there are stand-alone tools available for virtual world development, both open source and commercial.

Animation and Gesture Development Tools

In many projects you will want to take advantage of nonverbal communication features available in Second Life—gestures ("clap," "Hi," "Oh, no!" "nodding avatar's head," "scratching avatar's head in surprise," and similar short movements) and animations ("cat walk," "talking while gesticulating with both hands," "fiddling with avatar's hair and then looking at watch," and similar longer movements.)

Second Life comes with a library of common gestures and a built-in tool allowing you to join several existing gestures together, but if you want to create a lifelike simulation, you will often need to create new specific gestures and animations. There are several software packages that help you with this task, from commercial (3D Max from Autodesk, Adobe Director) and semicommercial (SketchUp from Google) to free (DAZ Studio, FreeCAD, Cyberdelia). We have had very good experiences with DAZ Studio (www.daz3d.com), although this software is so powerful that for the purpose of creating gestures and short animations, you use no more than 5 or 10 percent of its capabilities. A three-dimensional graphical user interface allows you to create a gesture by simply moving and rotating extremities of a 3-D "model," recording the position of all parts of the model's body at time points that you select, and saving the new gesture. After it is done, you export the newly created gesture as a BioVision File (extension *.bvh) and upload this file into Second Life. That is it—you have a new gesture in Second Life that you can apply to your avatar or to a robotic avatar to make the simulations you are working on more natural.

The only problem with the gestures is that at the moment Second Life does not support movements of fingers (an avatar can move only a palm of the hand simultaneously) and lip synchronization, but with the speed that virtual worlds advance, these features should be available in future versions.

Three-Dimensional Modeling Tools

One of the limitations you face in Second Life and other virtual worlds is the number of prims that you can have in any given area. A prim is a single-part object, the simplest indivisible "atomic" building block of a virtual world. A sphere, a cube, and a cylinder are all examples of prims. Primitives can be joined together to create complex objects.

In 2008 Second Life introduced a new type of primitive—a sculptured prim. In simple terms, it allows you to create a primitive object with a complex surface. Sculpted prims are used to create shapes that were not previously possible within Second Life. A mushroom, a car fender, a lighting fixture, or a back of an ergonomic chair can be created as a single prim, for example.

While relatively simple and "rough" objects are easy to produce using a built-in object editing tool, complex and more refined items, especially accurate models of real-life objects, are often created using stand-alone 3-D modeling software such as 3D Max, Maya, or Blender. If you want to use sculptured prims, you *have* to use a stand-alone program, since there are no in-world tools that would allow you to do that. Second Life wiki lists quite a few programs, both free and commercial (http://wiki.second life.com/wiki/Sculpted_Prims:_3d_Software_Guide) that you can use to create 3-D objects and, specifically, sculptured prims. If you are already using one of these programs, you can export your 3-D objects and use them in Second Life.

Regardless of the brand of software that you are using, in order to make 3-D objects available in Second Life, you should save them as "UV image" in a TGA format and then upload that image into Second Life. (A short explanation is in order: "UV image" means that you will create a map where a form of the object is encoded by color. TGA is simply a lossless graphical format. Unlike other graphical formats, such as JPEG or BMP that might be more familiar to you, it saves colors without errors or simplifications. Since in 3-D modeling colors correspond to the form of an object, using a TGA format ensures that the form is saved correctly.)

Inventory Management and Backup Tools

One of the most reliable ways to lose sleep is *not* to have backups of your computer work. A great way *not* to get the best possible return from your work is to keep materials disorganized. Up until recently, you could organize your Second Life inventory only inside Second Life. Even though Linden

Lab backs up all Second Life accounts and islands, many of us prefer to have our own backups, especially since it helps in organizing and managing different projects. Thanks to the Second Life My Inventory Viewer (SLMIV) project (www.joeswammi.com/sl/se/), there is a possibility to do this.

When you visit Second Life, the viewer creates a special file on your computer. This file is your complete My Inventory list. SLMIV allows you to work with this file: you can view detailed information about objects in your inventory; back up scripts, note cards, textures, and other images in your inventory; export inventory to an XML file; and review all sales, permissions, and key information associated with an inventory object, etc. Backing up this information onto a hard drive on your network or a flash drive allows you not only to save your work but to keep several versions that might come in handy later.

Communication Tools

There are several ways to communicate in a virtual world. The most common device is a text chat. Live voice communications between users are also possible and have been recently implemented in the Second Life world. As a backup for voice communication, many people use Skype (www.skype.com). There are several added benefits to using Skype:

▶ You can conference in people outside Second Life and even those away from a computer, since Skype allows calls to regular phone numbers around the world.

▶ You can easily record conference calls, meetings, and lectures using Skype plug-ins such as PrettyMay (www.prettymay.net).

▶ Using Simplecast (www.spacialaudio.com) or a similar program, you can stream (upload in real time) your Second Life audio to an audio server and rebroadcast it on the Web for a practically unlimited audience, as well as record it for future use.

Speaking about communication, we have to mention instant messaging, which has become an exceedingly popular means of communication. Thanks to bridging software such as the instant messaging (IM) program available from Comverse (www.comverse.com), you can IM between settings in a virtual world and mobile phones.

Rich Media in Virtual Worlds

The first foray into a rich media environment often starts with creating slides for presentations. In Second Life it requires little effort. To show PowerPoint slides, you first need to save them as graphic files in JPEG, or PNG format (PNG generally provides better quality). These images can be displayed as "textures" on any prim surface in-world. You will need to do a little programming for that, although many free or almost free "slide screens" are available in Second Life.

Similarly, video and animations can be projected onto a surface of a prim. Most often, such prims are created in the form of a flat screen with controls similar to those of a VCR or DVD player in real life. The video file is hosted on a server outside Second Life. Software is responsible for streaming it into Second Life and onto the surface of the prim when a user clicks "play." These screens can also be obtained from numerous vendors in Second Life.

Audio files provide more variety to a virtual world. You can play them using two methods:

▶ Similarly to video files, audio files can be kept on a server outside Second Life and streamed into Second Life on demand, triggered by clicking on a programmed object. This is most appropriate for large/long files, such as a recorded presentation.

▶ Small audio files can be uploaded into Second Life and played directly there, without needing to stream audio from an outside server. This method is most appropriate for small files used to create realistic simulations, such as a sound of a ringing telephone, a sound of working equipment, or a phrase to be "pronounced" by a robotic avatar.

Once you start using virtual worlds, you will find out that along with their direct use as a platform for training and other corporate activities inside virtual worlds, they provide an excellent platform for creating training *outside* virtual worlds. Creating video in a 3-D environment, called *machinimia*, is one of the important uses of virtual worlds, and Second Life provides built-in tools for recording video in-world. Since you already have the "studio" and the "actors," creating training videos or recording training sessions for future use and review by the next group of learners becomes a very time- and resource-effective solution. Among the third-party video solutions, CamStudio (www.camstudio.org) deserves your attention as an easy-to-use, high-quality, free software that will help you in recording your virtual world events.

In-World Training Solutions

As virtual worlds gain acceptance, vendors migrate from creating simple one-task tools, such as screens for slides and video, to creating complex instruments that more closely fall into the category of a "solution" rather than a "tool." For example, robotic avatars that appeared in mid-2008 grew into the Immersive Communication Training System (ICTS). Robotic avatars are used to provide training in all areas requiring communications, such as sales, customer service, price and terms negotiations with an outside vendor, manager-to-subordinate and subordinate-to-manager communications, and annual performance reviews. However, until recently, you had to work with programmers to create a simulation using robotic avatars. ICTS added a graphical user interface that allows instructional designers to create and modify a complex simulation without knowing programming or writing a single line of code.

Other in-world solutions allow organizations to carry out teamwork testing and training, conduct leadership training, test how well a person will perform under pressure, and perform other common types of training and testing.

Learning Management and Assessment Tools

If virtual worlds are to be used successfully as learning environments, training departments will need tools to manage learning offerings and assess the results of the training. As we already mentioned, a qualified programmer can connect Second Life simulations and tools to practically any outside database and learning management system. Sloodle is an example of such a tool. It is an open source project that combines the virtual Second Life environment with Moodle, an open source LMS. Learning management and assessment tools provided in Sloodle include a registration booth, an enrollment booth, an access checker, a course selector, live chat, a quiz creator, a glossary, and a vending machine.

In general, you should plan on connecting training, conferencing, Web, database, and other existing corporate tools to the virtual world systems you create. Existing technical capabilities certainly allow you to avoid duplication and make good use of the investment in technology that you already have.

First Steps in a Virtual World: Synchronous Training and Lectures

Synchronous training, when learners and instructor need to be in one location at the same time, often becomes the default first application of Second Life in corporate training. It seems to be an easy and logical step. However, you do need to take a few things into account to make it successful.

> "Order and simplification are the first steps toward mastery of a subject—the actual enemy is the unknown."
> —*Thomas Mann*

When you start a new project, you often begin with "training a trainer." Once you set up a location in Second Life, you need to train essential project personnel in using Second Life. With the wide popularity of Second Life, chances are some of the employees already have explored virtual worlds on their own and have their personal account. It seems to be logical to use these employees as core members of your Second Life project team. This is fine, as long as you follow a few precautions.

First, you probably want employees to keep business and personal affairs separate. In Second Life, this means creating a separate business account even for those employees who already have their own personal account and avatar. It pays to establish a policy of not using business avatars, especially if your business name is obvious from the avatar's name, for personal explorations of virtual worlds. In addition to eliminating potential business image problems, this policy makes bringing potentially nonsecure items and programs into your private region more difficult.

Second, having experience discovering virtual worlds as a hobby and being ready to take ownership of a corporate project are entirely different things. Just as being great at family cookouts does not qualify a person for running a successful restaurant, exploring Second Life for personal amusement is not enough to plan and execute a successful training or business project using this platform. The latter involves skills such as setting up valid business goals, planning, creating objects, programming, connecting Second Life to Web applications and databases, streaming sound and video technology, and other specific expertise. Often, an employee's experience with virtual worlds is lopsided toward entertainment and social interaction, which might not be the main features you want to explore as a company.

To be sure, having on staff people with any experience in Second Life comes in handy when you assemble a core team to help jump-start the project and create a bank of ideas. However, having seen a few disappointments attributable to a lack of business experience, inaccurate or erroneous targeting, tactical ineptness in technology, and, sometimes, a lack of strategic vision, in most cases we would recommend outsourcing for at least the technological and organizational parts of a virtual world project.

In many instances, you should consider engaging Second Life consultants to help define strategic goals and milestones as well. Of course, outsourcing never works as a "fire-and-forge" arrangement. Intel's experience (see the case study later in this chapter) suggests, among other things, that you need to make certain that there is a full understanding of the purpose and targets of your Second Life projects and the image you want to project. One of the questions to ask both employees and prospective contractors is, "Suppose we proceed with this project and create X, Y, and Z as you suggest. For those who have never been to Second Life, how would you describe the content and experience?"

An alternative approach was successfully tried by Microsoft (see the case study in this chapter) in building its developer community. When a Microsoft employee—the MSDN developer evangelist—decided to build and support a community of and for developers, he was alone. However, in Second Life he found a few similar-minded people. Together, they organized first meetings attended by just a few software specialists. A year after the community-building effort started, the developer community counts more than eight hundred members and is growing. Along with the professionals, it includes many end users. The whole community is self-organized—Microsoft employees do not manage it or play an administrative role.

The two examples have a lot in common. Since both Intel and Microsoft are leading technology companies, and both have used virtual worlds for similar types of projects, we can compare them in detail, as shown in Table 6.1.

 ## Intel Software Network Expands in Second Life: A Case Study

In a world of cutthroat competition, a technology company can survive only if it attracts enough outside developers to create business solutions based on its products. The best in the field are always looking to expand their networks by attracting new talent.

The Intel Software Network (ISN) was created as a Web-based platform to allow software developers to access Intel tools and technologies, as well as to help grow horizontal links among developers within a community-type structure. The network has really fostered developer communities working in all areas of computer technologies: from academic computing to mobile-aware applications to parallel and multi-core programming to XML processing.

TABLE 6.1

	Intel	*Microsoft*
Major uses	• Expansion of Intel Software Network • Building community of developers; main objectives: growing horizontal links between developers, self-help, exchange of ideas, technical support • New-product launches	• Building community of developers; main objectives: self-help, exchange of ideas, technical support • New-product launches
Project development	Outside contractor	Second Life community; developers with strong Second Life experience
Number of company employees involved	Informal and semiformal peer group of up to 20 people	1 to 10
Number of external developers active in the community on a regular basis	More than 600	More than 800
Number of external developers who simultaneously took part in onetime events (product launch, etc.)	More than 100	Up to 300
Day-to-day management	Intel employees	Leadership Council consisting of outside developers and Microsoft employees
Event management	Outside contractor	Outside contractor
Training program for employees and users	Yes	Yes
Employee virtual world code of conduct	Same as a regular online employee code of conduct	No official code of conduct
Realized cost avoidance	Privileged	Avoided 65 to 90 percent costs of similar real-life programs

	Intel	*Microsoft*
Plans for expansion of virtual world programs	Yes	Yes
Recommendations	• Manage expectations • Work with Second Life community and bloggers	• Do not wait; start exploring virtual worlds

Few people know this better then Paul Steinberg, a course architect at Intel. For more than eight years, Steinberg has been helping software developers and end users to work with Intel tools and technologies, developing and implementing training. Not surprisingly, Steinberg became an internal champion of virtual worlds as another venue to extend the reach of a vitally important network. The project began in Second Life. As it flourished, Intel also started experimenting with the OpenSim platform.

In spite of being a technology company, Intel chose to outsource most of the development to an outside contractor with extensive expertise in Second Life. As always, outsourcing proved to be a double-edged sword. The contractor had a great understanding of what works and what doesn't work in a virtual environment, and that helped to save resources. On the other hand, the contractor came into the project with a preconceived image of Intel as a large chip manufacturer and built the site accordingly. It took several iterations to change the content to what Intel really had in mind: to create an open community site as opposed to the chip manufacturer's site in Second Life. Development of the Second Life site, all expenses included, ran less than $100,000 and took approximately five months to complete.

When word about the Second Life project spread throughout the company, many people from outside the software network—and Steinberg's circle—reached out to him to participate in the program. Intel employees with personal experience in Second Life helped conceptualize ideas, reviewed site designs, and reached out to the Second Life community at large to promote the ISN project. One of the unexpected but highly welcome results of the project was the creation of an internal peer network that now helps with the virtual worlds initiative on an ad hoc basis. For the employees without prior hands-on experience with Second Life, Steinberg set up a semiformal training program. To keep things simple, Intel decided to use the same code of conduct that Intel employees adhere to when working on the Web in other capacities.

Because it is a highly interactive medium, Second Life is impossible to imagine without visual tools. ISN in Second Life used simple instruments to enhance communications. PowerPoint slides were converted to images and shown on a screen. Video clips were streamed simultaneously into Second Life and on the Web. Later, Intel started translating Second Life events to the Web, again increasing the reach of the developer's network.

More than six hundred developers connected to ISN in Second Life. Since many events were highly technical and narrowly specialized in nature, most of them were attended by groups of ten to twelve people, although ISN held several general events that were attended by more than one hundred developers at a time. Intel engineers who were leading technical events were always surprised by the depth of questions and high level of technical expertise among community members who were taking part in Second Life events.

Prior to Second Life, Intel had used webinars for similar programs. Compared to webinars and even live meetings, Second Life events led to far more meaningful and deep conversations. Audiences would get deeply involved and start side conversations using instant messaging, texting, and voice. These conversations would involve the whole audience as well as the featured speakers. This kind of highly productive conversation is almost impossible to have during a webinar or even a live meeting in the physical world. In the real world, a side conversation among several attendees immediately becomes a disruptive nuisance.

The organizers saw that the availability of several modes of conversation provided a unique opportunity for a "multidimensional" simultaneous exchange. That allowed Intel to realize its business objective of building a highly active developer community to a greater depth than would otherwise be possible. This is especially interesting because the cost of engagement per developer was slightly less in Second Life than it would have been using alternative technologies. Scaling (ability to seamlessly increase the number of users as needed) also noticeably decreases the cost of engagement and thus increases attractiveness of the virtual world program.

As with most other corporate projects in Second Life, Intel had to answer several important challenges. Among the problems organizations often face when considering virtual world technologies, the most important are network security and dealing with so-called griefers—people who disrupt somebody else's work as a form of entertainment and self-assertion. The larger the organization or event they can cause grief to, the prouder they are.

There were a limited number of "griefing" attempts, and those that did happen were opportunistic, not premeditated. For large events Intel hired outside firms to help with crowd management and security. They provided preregistration, created access lists, and managed access and "crowd control." That helped to avoid severe cases of event disruption. In general, Steinberg's advice is to treat griefers as adolescents (which, in many cases, they actually are) looking to attract attention.

When it comes to network security, Intel is in a much better position than most other companies; after all, it is their area of expertise! A corporate internal network security team ran a series of tests on Second Life and concluded that it is as secure as an average Web application. Perhaps this is another important side result of the Intel project. We can hardly imagine better-qualified network security specialists, and we believe that their opinion carries a lot of weight for potential corporate Second Life clients.

For the pilot project, Intel decided to increase security by allowing Second Life applications to be run only through the "guest" network, which is available for company visitors and is not connected to the internal network or protected by the enterprise firewall. A version of Second Life software that will run on a stand-alone server behind a corporate firewall will probably widen corporate acceptance by eliminating network security concerns.

Finally, a word to the wise: here's what Intel would have done differently, given its current experience.

First, Steinberg recommends careful managing of expectations. In a large organization there are many stakeholders, and it is important to have a single vision. You will need plenty of patience building this vision, as there are no turnkey solutions in virtual worlds. To achieve optimal results, Steinberg recommends that you be open about your goals, your intentions, and the ways you want to achieve them.

When Intel announced its plans, it received extensive negative publicity from bloggers who assumed that a large company will do something (or everything) wrong when executing an initiative such as this. Of course, these bloggers had no idea what Intel's long-term plans and goals were. Intel answered by reaching out directly to the community, providing information, and explaining what they really wanted to do and why. Open conversation with adversaries, be it adolescent griefers or middle-aged bloggers, worked well for Intel, and Steinberg recommends that you employ this strategy as well.

Unlike a website, a Second Life project is never complete; it always keeps growing and changing. Today, Intel looks at its virtual worlds strategy with an eye toward expanding both external and intraorganizational projects. The company views virtual worlds as a very important part of the Intel strategy and encourages other companies to get engaged with this new technology. It is its belief that virtual worlds will change the way business deals with people, with networks, with information, and with data—and Intel will be at the forefront of this shift.

Self-Directed Developer Community: A Case Study of Microsoft's Experience in Second Life

While Microsoft is arguably the best-known software company in the world, the public often does not realize how much the company's success depends on the hard work of the many independent developers who create custom solutions based on Microsoft tools. Microsoft's reputation, in many ways, rests on the satisfaction of these developers with Microsoft's products and its support services.

When Zain Naboulsi of Microsoft started experimenting with Second Life, he looked at it not as a project with fixed start and completion dates but as a forward-looking effort with the vision of creating a base to build and support a community of dedicated developers. The community would be a place for existing developers to meet and discuss their ideas, as well as a way to attract new talent. During the year, Microsoft also supported several major events in Second Life that attracted significantly more developers: C# Day, Visual Studio 2008 Service Pack 1 Launch, and the Heroes Happen Here Launch.

Initially, Naboulsi was the only Microsoft employee tasked with implementing this vision, but as the project evolved and succeeded in attracting an increasing target audience, he was joined by eight to ten people ranging in level from a software developer to an executive.

While Naboulsi entered Second Life alone, he looked for and found "seed" developers, to whom he proposed the idea of conducting regular user group meetings. .NET developer Tori Ashe shared the idea with others, and three people showed up at the first meeting of the inaugural .NET Users Group. Then and there, they decided to keep moving forward regardless of how many people might show up for future meetings. Today, a year after the community-building effort started, there are more than eight hundred active developers, system administrators, and end users taking part in regular meetings of eight product-specific groups (.NET Users Group, IT Pro Users Group, Visual Studio Team System Users Group, SQL PASS Chapter, Microsoft Office Users Group, LSL Scripting Users Group, Developer Round Table Sessions, and Code Clinic Sessions).

We must commend Microsoft for its courage: the company trusted "outsiders" to build a community that in many respects defines Microsoft's face in the software community at large. Company employees played only a supporting role.

This courage paid off. Unpaid enthusiasts developed the highly successful .NET Developers Island. Microsoft provided only the island itself as a base for the community activities, at an annual cost of $2,340. The leadership council that is now in place determines the schedules, events, and general direction of all future activities, making these activities more relevant to the needs of the developers while reducing the load on the company employees.

Interestingly, Microsoft employees are prohibited from becoming officers in any user group and cannot make decisions about the island by themselves. The only exception to this rule is a "veto right" reserved for Zain Naboulsi—one he has never used and expects that he will not need to use in the future.

But what about security or "griefers" trying to interrupt meetings? As the never-ending war with computer viruses shows, there are plenty of malicious attackers who consider disrupting the work of a high-profile company a special badge of honor. Since neither Microsoft nor the community itself prescreens people who wish to join the project, one would expect ongoing security issues.

Wrong! To the surprise of many, the project has had only one serious issue: someone spammed the sandbox with pornographic materials. (Side note: "sandbox" in Second Life lingo is an area where anybody is allowed to build, create models, and create and run scripts. These activities are generally limited or prohibited outside the sandbox area. If you provide a sandbox, it is a good idea to automatically "clean" it daily or more often.) Interestingly, some people who have experience with Second Life consider the availability of a sandbox to be mandatory for a project's success. Microsoft's experience proves otherwise. Immediately after the security incident, the sandbox was removed. Later, sandboxes were reinstated but placed in the sky (you need to know of their existence and their coordinates to be able to teleport there), and access is now limited to officers and select user group members.

Generally, security infractions are successfully handled by the community itself without Microsoft needing to interfere. To date only four people have been banned from the island due to security violations. It is worth noting that there is no official code of conduct. Perhaps the fact that this is a community of similar-minded people with the same interests contributed to the creation of an environment highly conducive to learning and participation, which discourages disruptive behavior.

Since the island has become a multibranch venue, users need to have a good handle on the multiple tools that are available in Second Life. They have access to in-world instant messaging, voice communications, slide viewers, scripts, and other tools. Training in using an environment that was new to some users turned out to be a good idea. Training helped newcomers to avoid confusion and allowed them to promptly take a meaningful role in the community activities. Most of the learning happens informally, with more experienced members of the peer group helping novices, but there are also various classes that offer help as well.

According to the overwhelmingly positive feedback of the growing community, the only thing that can beat the 3-D experience in Second Life is meeting in the physical world. However, according to Microsoft, the cost of engagements in Second Life is about one-tenth the cost of conducting user group meetings in the real world.

In the case of events that attract more people, the relative costs are higher but still only about one-third of an equivalent physical world event. The lower ROI for larger events in Second Life is due to limitations on the number of people you can put on one island in Second Life at the same time. This capacity is gradually but constantly increasing. For the time being, to circumvent this limitation, for large events Microsoft temporarily rents three additional islands to handle the load. Because between two and three hundred people, on average, take part in these events, Microsoft also hires temporary help at a cost of $4,000 per event to prepare facilities on the rented land quickly and to help with the event management.

It is interesting to note that in spite of lower cost avoidance (although the company still realized 65 to 70 percent savings!) these were one-day events for outside developers, not Microsoft employees. Correspondingly, when calculating comparative costs of events in the physical world (rent, food, etc.) we do not include the incidentals, such as travel and lodging, that would make savings when holding an intracompany event even higher.

Naboulsi has just one regret about bringing Microsoft into Second Life: "My only regret is that I didn't do this sooner. I won't say doing things in this space is easy by any means, but it is very rewarding for the community." In 2009 Microsoft plans to expand the project into other virtual worlds such as OpenSim.

Conclusions and Best Practices

In spite of different approaches to virtual worlds, both Intel and Microsoft achieved significant success in reaching their major goal: building a Second Life community of independent developers who work with their products. Developers actively use these communities for self-help, exchange of ideas, technical support, and building horizontal links with their peers.

Since Microsoft works with a larger group of developers, it is not surprising that its Second Life community includes more members. In fact, given the highly specialized qualities and much smaller overall number of Intel developers, we are surprised that the difference is not higher. The difference between the two companies in their approaches to building a community can also be attributed to their specialization; it is probably easier to find a Microsoft developer in Second Life (or other virtual worlds for that matter) than to find an Intel developer.

One way or another, both companies definitely achieved success and enhanced their leadership positions in the industry. Their experience provides a good road map in starting synchronous training, lectures, and community-building efforts in virtual worlds. Based on their information and experience, we can summarize the following as best practices:

► Do not mix business and pleasure; create a separate business account for all employees even if they already have a Second Life account.

► Employees with prior experience in Second Life may be a great source of ideas. Consider all possible resources for developing your Second Life location, including employees and contractors. Take into account the skills and experience necessary for building, programming, and day-to-day management. A contractor will better handle specialized tasks, such as large events.

► Build semiformal and informal networks both inside and outside the organization. Self-help and peer-to-peer training is often the most effective type of learning, especially in Second Life.

► Use Second Life tools to facilitate multichannel collaboration (simultaneous use of voice, chat, and instant messaging).

► Create visual tools, taking advantage of the Second Life environment.

► If your project targets outside developers, users, or customers, do not be afraid to form joint "employee-plus-outsiders" groups or councils that will reach out to your target audience and help you manage the project.

Teaching Complex Concepts in a New Way: The Michelin Group Case Study

Written by Philippe Barreaud and Alex Heiphetz

What do *you* think when somebody mentions Michelin? Most people probably think of tires and the world-famous mascot, the Michelin Man, while for some, the Michelin Red Guide for hotels and restaurants will come to mind. But, those who know the industry think "innovation."

> " It's a simple concept, but a complex system."
> —*David Rice,*
> *CEO of Haywood*
> *Regional Medical Center,*
> *North Carolina*

Michelin is a global tire manufacturer with seventy-five factories and a commercial presence in 170 countries. Founded in 1889 by André and Edouard Michelin in the Auvergne region of France, Michelin has a long history of "firsts": the first removable bicycle tire, the first car equipped with tires, the first radial tire. Its unique guidebook for drivers in 1900 at a time when information was scarce was perhaps the first "information technology" project in the industry.

Innovation is still driving the company today. In 1992 Michelin started introducing silica to the rubber compound used to produce tires, lowering rolling resistance and reducing fuel consumption and carbon dioxide emissions. In addition to product innovation, the company continues to offer new services. For example, fleet managers can now purchase Michelin tires based on miles actually driven rather than by the unit, an innovation that supports a sustainable development model.

As a market leader, the company is facing intense competition from both traditional rivals and new market entrants. In answering these challenges, Michelin accelerates innovation, cuts cycle times, reduces costs, and maintains a steady growth around the world.

Michelin also needs to consider its new "global customers" and meet their expectations: car manufacturers are increasingly designing their vehicles at a single location and manufacturing them in a different location for several markets around the world. A flexible global supply chain is mandatory to meet customer demand.

In response, the company developed a strong process approach across its various business units to define global standard processes and leverage best practices across the organization. This approach created the foundation of a global delivery model for information systems (IS) solutions by:

▶ Focusing resources on building/deploying standard solutions in support of the new global processes
▶ Implementing a worldwide delivery organization
▶ Leveraging partnerships with suppliers to improve productivity and accelerate production cycles

It became critical to ensure that everyone along the design and production chain of information systems (IS) solutions understood their tasks in the context of Michelin's enterprise architecture (EA). The challenge was to train two hundred IS professionals in the United States, Europe, and Asia whose job was to design and deliver appropriate solutions. They needed to understand Michelin's enterprise architecture and be able to translate the EA deliverables into practical standard solutions that would work in the field.

The bad news is that all traditional training approaches failed. The feedback was unanimous: "too many concepts," "not practical," and "difficult to understand." This universal rejection of the training method jeopardized Michelin's goal of having IS employees appreciate the need for a global alignment of processes and IS solutions.

Because everything else had failed, the information systems department looked for alternative ways to solve the problem. A virtual world–based program seemed like the most practical solution, and choosing Second Life from among other virtual worlds was a "no-brainer" at the time, since other virtual world solutions were practically nonexistent. The company was looking for an environment that could satisfy two training scenarios: (1) a small team of people attending a scheduled course under the supervision of an instructor, and (2) a place for individual trainees to come back regularly for practice after attending the course.

 ## Training Delivery

Once the Michelin training center in Second Life had been created (Figure 7.1), the introduction of the new technology and training was a gradual, multistep process.

First, trainees were invited to attend a session with an instructor in a room equipped with PCs running Second Life. (The company wanted to avoid the risk of trainees struggling on their own with a new technology without access to immediate assistance.) At this point, trainees were given pre-created avatars. At the end of the course, trainees were given instructions on how to create their own avatars and how to install the Second Life client on their workstations. They received necessary clearance to access Second Life and enter the Michelin islands.

Very important, trainees also received a list of technical support contacts. At this point they were ready to pursue their own training path. The architecture of the actual building where Michelin conducted training matched that of the Second Life buildings that trainees saw when they entered the island. The company had used a location away from the office, conducive to learning. But at the same time, the Second Life environment

FIGURE 7.1

carried a subtle familiarity to bridge the gap between real life and the virtual premises.

As a training canvas, Michelin used one of three close-to-reality scenarios. After the initial introduction to enterprise architecture and basic skills necessary in Second Life, trainees had to build an EA for one of the following (Figure 7.2):

- ▶ A community planing to increase educational and cultural public services
- ▶ A community planning to become more attractive to businesses
- ▶ A community looking for the ways to become environmentally friendly

The first step was to build the business architecture for the selected scenario. During this step trainees went through a sequence of three workshops (Figure 7.3) where they learned:

FIGURE 7.2

FIGURE 7.3

1. How to select business targets consistent with the scenario they had chosen
2. How to build business processes to reach their goals
3. How to group process elements into clusters that are meaningful in terms of business or information systems actions or solutions

The exercises for this first step are interactive; trainees select objects and assemble them into deliverables. For instance, they build processes with process elements provided to them, further developing their Second Life skills (Figure 7.4).

During the second step, trainees define the IS architecture for their scenario. They learn how to delineate relevant IS services covering the business processes they defined during the previous step and how to regroup these IS services into applications. These exercises are even more interactive than those in the previous step.

FIGURE 7.4

The third step is to create a road map for developing and installing the applications (Figure 7.5). Applications defined in Step 2 exist in several versions with increased functional improvements. Trainees must assemble a road map to their business targets while not exceeding budget constraints. Step 3 is the most interactive. Standing in front of a matrix, trainees must place applications on the map correctly. The exercise is constructed in such a manner that those who didn't pay attention in the virtual class and might try a semi-random trial-and-error approach would eventually succeed in building a working road map, but it would take so much time that they would get a failing grade. After completion of Step 3, trainees review a presentation on the connection between enterprise architecture and governance.

The all-inclusive cost of preparing the training environment in Second Life was €60,000 (approximately $100,000 at the time) or €300 (approxi-

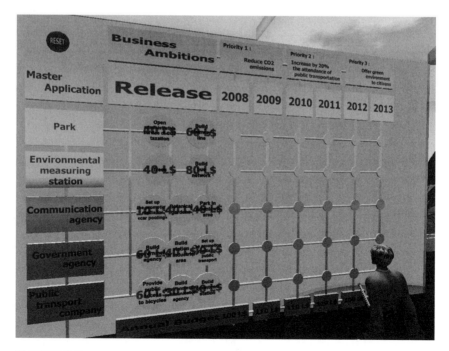

FIGURE 7.5

mately $500) per trainee. Second Life training was noticeably more productive and effective. There was a clear reduction in training time, as well as a significant improvement in quality, learning results, user acceptance, and user satisfaction.

User Feedback

Across all countries, feedback was overwhelmingly positive. Table 7.1 presents responses as percentages based on 163 completed feedback forms (Figure 7.6).

TABLE 7.1

	I understand the EA methodology (% of respondents)	*Second Life appropriate to learn about EA (% of respondents)*
Very true	60.7	59.5
True	35.6	38.0
Somewhat true	3.7	2.5
Not true	0	0

User acceptance did not vary according to background or culture. Following are some typical responses received from Michelin employees from around the world:

THAILAND

"I enjoyed the virtual training most. It is very interesting. Better than the standard training we had before."

"Should be applied to other training."

"We can learn and understand the EA process within half a day which is unbelievable."

"Made learning enjoyable."

FIGURE 7.6

CHINA

"Enjoyed the way of doing presentations and exercises."

"Very good tool that gives the information in an exciting way."

"Not boring."

"Very interactive, cool technology."

"Clear picture of the EA phases and practice to apply the concepts."

"I enjoyed using games to understand the principles."

EUROPE

"SL interactivity enabled me to stay focused on the EA approach."

"Made a complex topic simple and understandable."

UNITED STATES

"SL enhanced the training giving virtual breaks."

"Interactivity with the medium encouraged attention."

"SL kept me engaged and interested in what could have been a very boring subject."

COMMENT FROM CHIEF ARCHITECT

"Interestingly, what appeared more obvious with time was the fact that we had packaged a lot of interactive workshops into a short period of time, which would have been impossible to do in real life. The training delivery was efficient—i.e., we made the best of the trainees' time and productivity; i.e., they really understood the EA approach and how to apply it."

Hardware and Security Issues

When you think of deploying a virtual world–based training program, it is important to verify basic technical capabilities. For Michelin it proved essential to test the standard PCs that the company had to ensure that they would be able to run the Second Life client. On some of the computers, technicians had to update graphical card drivers.

Another important issue the company considered was security. Michelin's approach has been two-pronged:

▶ Michelin, working with IBM, created an access gateway. Users have to sign in to use Second Life from their corporate PCs. Access rights to the gateway are managed in the same manner as for any other system.

▶ Michelin islands in Second Life are "private"; users' avatars must be authorized to enter the island.

Lessons Learned

Virtual world training offers some key advantages compared to other types of media:

▶ Paradoxically, it is easy to create "reality" in a virtual world; the hands-on workshops helped trainees understand the concepts more fully and allowed for immediate feedback.

▶ Total immersion invoked an intense gamelike passion: trainees would not leave until they had completed all the exercises. Competition among trainees added to the fun, at the same time intensifying learning and sustaining employee attention in a way that is difficult to achieve in a real-world training session.

▶ Second Life allowed Michelin's training staff to pack a lot of interactive learning experiences within a very short amount of time, cutting training time. The Michelin experience demonstrates that training in virtual worlds can be more efficient than in other training venues. The training experience is often more intense and makes better use of trainees' time through training automation.

Because training efficiency is a relevant key performance indicator, Philippe Barreaud, chief enterprise architect, proposed the following productivity indicator:

$$(T_{VW} - T_{PW}) / T_{PW}$$

where T_{VW} is time required to complete training in a virtual world and T_{PW} is time it would take to deliver the same training, with the same level of hands-on experience, in the physical world.

What Could Have Been Done Differently?

Experience demonstrated that all trainees, regardless of their age, country of residence, and technical background, acquired Second Life skills faster than Michelin had planned. The company could have been less cautious and organized training sessions with more attendees, as the amount of supervision needed was less than originally anticipated. Michelin, at this point, did not test the possibility of 100 percent virtual remote training. The company anticipates migrating in this direction in the future.

Conclusions and Best Practices

The results of the Michelin experience can be summarized as the following best practices:

- ▶ Experiencing firsthand rather than conceptualizing, and being part of a story that is happening right now rather than being a passive reader of slides, leads to a feeling of engagement in the project and of making progress. This, however, requires new skills on the part of an educator, who becomes more of a conductor of an orchestra than a lecturer.

- ▶ Break your training into parts and use different ways to deliver the message depending on what is most appropriate for each part.

- ▶ Working in a virtual world means making the training path as visual and obvious as possible: use arrows, floor arrows, and sky tracers to indicate the correct direction of movement and the path that needs to be followed from one exercise to another.

- ▶ Keeping presentations flowing from one exhibit (slide, movie, workshop) to another keeps participants fully engaged, encouraging them to stay on topic.

▶ Create opportunities for trainees to interact with one another in the virtual world. Encourage situations where trainees have to team up to do an exercise. Include a forum for scheduled lectures and discussions.

▶ There are three recommended methods for working with traditional slideshows in Second Life:
1. Have slide panels where users can click on a small slide to scale it up to see the details.
2. Display slides as billboards along the training path so that trainees discover them as they "walk the presentation" (Figure 7.7).
3. Use more traditional slideshows that you can project on a screen during a presentation (Figure 7.8).

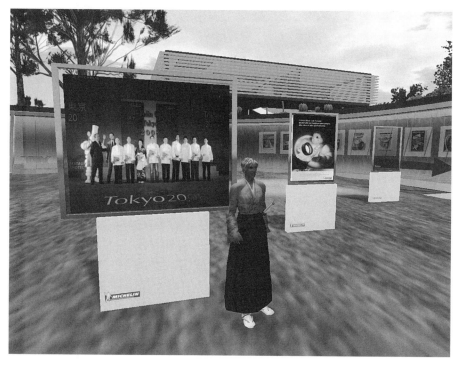

FIGURE 7.7

FIGURE 7.8

▶ Interactive tools that trainees can operate by themselves are a great way to increase their understanding, participation, and buy-in (Figure 7.9).

▶ Use tools such as a whiteboard for feedback as well as interactivity.

▶ Start with a well-defined project with:
  – a discernable start and finish
  – key performance indicators (KPIs) to measure success; use real KPIs for training in a virtual world
  – a manageable number of participants at any given moment in the virtual space (perhaps fifteen to twenty)
  – project team members who are passionate about what they are doing

FIGURE 7.9

–classroom sessions to mitigate the risk of using a new technology

–a review of the hardware, bandwidth, and security issues before starting

–a great vendor who can develop and maintain the virtual environment and the tools you will need inside the environment, and offer technical support to your users

▶ Do not leave users to fend for themselves in a virtual world. Use instructors, robotic avatars, and tools to support your learners.

▶ A mix of self-training (with an instructor close by—just in case), group sessions, and debriefing/question sessions is a good way to leverage the virtual environment in as many ways as possible and to maximize an impact.

▶ Bridge the virtual world and the physical world. Use browser windows to display physical world applications whenever relevant. Include gateways to link with online resources as well as places where users can submit questions or comments via e-mail or browse relevant intranet/ Internet sites.

▶ Beware that overly ambitious initiatives often fail. Forces against change can be too strong and a technology will not necessarily scale well at the early stages of its development.

▶ Provide trainees with tools for self-assessment and monitoring their progress.

▶ Measure new knowledge with objective metrics, and analyze training efficiency with quizzes and tests.

▶ Create badges and other fun stuff, and award trainees when they complete an exercise or win a contest. Create a "Hall of Fame" for the trainees, measure the trainees' satisfaction, and receive their feedback on possible improvements. Create a fun space where people can have a break from training—an exhibition of fun facts from the company's history, or a racing track, for instance.

▶ Create a short movie inside the virtual world, and use it to advertise the course.

▶ Test, test, and test again; bugs can discourage trainees quickly.

▶ Link virtual world training to the company's HR training records. Keep it simple. Count virtual world training the same as all other types of training for HR purposes.

▶ Include a training passport that records the modules that trainees have completed and the results that they have achieved.

Michelin is one the first industrial companies that took the risk of investing in a significant training program in Second Life and was rewarded with major success. Several aspects make this success especially important:

▶ Second Life training succeeded where other training methodologies failed.

▶ Success was achieved while the costs went down. Once Michelin had established a base in Second Life, the company needed very limited funds to support the project for further use.

Besides the success of the project itself, Michelin gained increased recognition from its peers. The Second Life training project won a first award in the education category during the 2008 "Jules Verne" edition of the Intraverse contest (Figure 7.10). Intraverse awards are bestowed by an

FIGURE 7.10

international panel of experts for the best 3-D projects proven to deliver tangible value. Michelin also won a second "Special Jury Prize" Intraverse award during IMAGINA 2009 in Monaco for "outstanding achievements in sustainable innovation in virtual worlds." The Michelin project was also presented with a Silver World Intraverse Award in London on May 7, 2009.

Teamwork and Leadership in Virtual Worlds

Organizations that have improved the teamwork skills of their workers report significant benefits: reduced costs, conflicts, and absenteeism; increased employee involvement; enhanced innovation; and better adaptability and flexibility in the organization. At the same time, many employees think teamwork training is a fad. They describe it as a necessary evil and see their coworkers as simply interested in protecting their own turf. Conducting teamwork and leadership training in a nonthreatening, highly interactive environment of a virtual world helps change this attitude.

> "Effective leaders are not preachers; they are doers."
>
> —*Peter Drucker, founder of modern management theory*

Teamwork Training in Virtual Worlds

All course outlines for team training look mostly the same. Invariably, they list such items as "Building Team Trust" (remember the stunt of falling backward on your teammates' hands parodied in a GEICO insurance ad?), "Team Survey" (a survey to help learners identify their team player style), "Parker's Characteristics" (twelve characteristics of effective teams as developed by Glenn Parker), and others. These courses have been taught for decades, often successfully, but nevertheless they do have one serious shortcoming. They are taught through a combination of lectures, small group work, and case studies, where participants work in small groups to discuss the strengths and weaknesses of their teamwork.

We think that such theoretical study, important as it is, should definitely take a backseat to procedural knowledge. Working as a successful team, or being a real leader, requires skills, practice, and experience that simply cannot be learned entirely through lectures and case studies. Traditionally, the most successful courses on teamwork include synchronous in-class role-playing and teamwork-building activities to supplement theoretical knowledge, which is why virtual worlds are so well suited for team building. As we show here, teamwork simulations in virtual worlds can replace synchronous face-to-face exercises and offer many advantages beyond saving time and money on travel.

Initially, virtual worlds were used as a platform for real-time synchronous role-play exercises, including teamwork activities. Development of programming techniques made it possible to employ both synchronous and asynchronous simulations in virtual worlds. These simulations let existing and prospective team members test and be tested on their teamwork IQ, as well as learn their strengths and weaknesses in a real, but—and this is extremely important—nonthreatening environment. According to Jay Cross with coauthors (Cross et al. 2006), some of the features that help virtual worlds to support immersive experiential learning include learning by doing, engagement, repetition (ability to try as many times as learners choose), and the ability to observe others and to mix inactivity and challenge in the right proportions. All these features result in learners' motivation, which in turn translates into better training results.

We can add to this mixture a semi-scientific concept of "fun." As Will Glass (2005) noted, a quality of fun, while perhaps not a precise scientific term, is a very important parameter in how well a simulation works. Well-thought-out and well-constructed simulations are fun to use. Learners feel as if they are playing, not going through another marginally relevant assignment forced upon them by management. As a result, the skills and knowledge that a person receives during the simulation "stick"—the outcome that training professionals strive to achieve and which is so hard to achieve by the other methods.

Virtual World vs. Real-Life Simulations

Generally, virtual world teamwork and leadership simulations imitate relatively simple real-world situations which, in order to be completed, require the coordinated work of several people. A simulation scenario may include solving a puzzle, building a model of a house, or going through an obstacle course, to name a few.

You can create a similar training simulation in the physical world, for example, by asking several learners to solve a jigsaw puzzle. There are several obvious disadvantages to running this type of simulation in the physical world and one perhaps less obvious but very important downside. The obvious shortcomings include potential problems with accessing the simulation by several (usually four to six) people who need to work simultaneously, and the requirement that all of the learners need to be at the same location at the same time. A less obvious but more important downside of a real-life simulation of this kind is the inability to record who did what—which learner worked most productively, who interfered with the work of others, who demonstrated good teamwork skills and leadership qualities, and who needs to pay more attention to his or her teammates.

Unlike physical world simulations, those in virtual worlds can be designed and built to collect complete information on individual and team performance. Anything that happens digitally can be measured and recorded. As Lord Kelvin famously noted, "To measure is to know . . . if you can not measure it, you can not improve it."

It's a good idea to keep the records of all raw (unprocessed) data in a database outside the virtual world. You can process these records to extract valuable information on performance at any time after the simulation is completed. Since you have access to unprocessed data, you can always return to it later and reprocess it using different methods and programs, according to your needs.

Examples of Teamwork Simulations in Virtual Worlds

One of the available teamwork simulations in virtual worlds—Teamwork Tester—uses an assignment of solving a puzzle by several trainees as a model for teaching and testing teamwork skills (Heiphetz and Liberman 2007). The simulation is built on the Second Life platform. It consists of nine cubes with elements of six pictures on their sides. After one of the trainees scrambles the puzzle, all participants are free to select any cube and rotate it around three axes using keyboard controls (Figure 8.1). The objective is to complete the puzzle (to put together any one of the six images) as quickly as possible without any verbal or text communication among the members of the group. It does not matter which image a team puts together—the point of the simulation is for the team members to adjust their work to the work of others and work on the same image. The better the team is, the faster its members realize what image is being put together and start working on the pieces of the image their teammates are putting together. Members of the dysfunctional teams have a tendency to insist that others follow their lead, trying to "force" their selections on their teammates.

A somewhat similar simulation is described by O'Connell and coauthors (2009). The subjects in the research, conducted using the PanelPuzzle simulation, had to locate puzzle pieces that were placed "throughout a city, inside and outside buildings. Each puzzle piece had a random numerical identifier. Pieces also indicated the size of the panels to which they belonged. After finding a piece, players asked the GM [game master] to insert it into a specific section of a panel."

The principal difference between the two simulations is the role that authors assigned to communication. As described earlier, the groups that

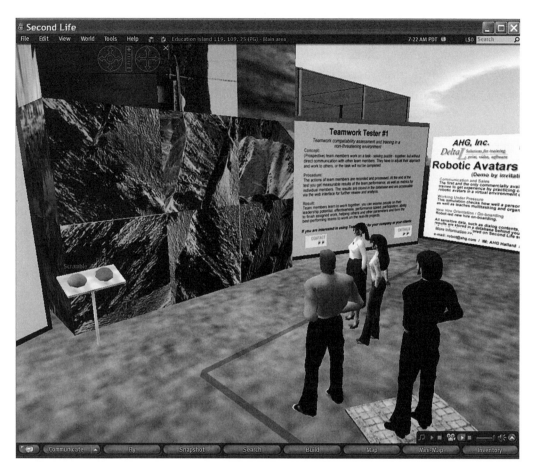

FIGURE 8.1

worked with Teamwork Tester were prevented from using verbal or text communications. Once the simulation started, all members of the group could work on the puzzle at the same time. They could not, however, communicate and decide beforehand what image they were going to put together. Members of the "efficient" teams would quickly determine which image was being put together by their teammates and adjust their work to build the image that had been already started. They completed the assignment quickly, without interfering with the work of other team members, but providing help when necessary—just as a good team would do working on any real-life task. Often such teams would have a clear leader who would initiate the pattern and others would quickly follow his or her lead.

In a group with poor teamwork, individual members would work on their own chosen image, often paying little attention to what others were doing, or even interfering with their work, "destroying" cubes their team-mates had already put in the "correct" position. Again, it was not important *which* image was completed; the task was to build *any* image in the shortest time possible. In "dysfunctional" teams, the cubes would be switched back and forth to different images by different members of the team, and the task stalled without any noticeable progress. Sometimes, observers could see two or more apparent leaders literally fighting for the leadership role and destroying an almost completed puzzle in order to force the rest of the team to follow their direction. Of course, these are extreme cases, and most often the real-life teams fall somewhere in between.

In the PanelPuzzle simulation (O'Connell et al. 2009), players had a choice of communication tools; in fact, communication was an important aspect of the simulation. The participants could communicate with each other and simultaneously with the game master (the researcher conducting the experiment) using text chat or by exchanging messages through a forum. Players also could communicate by voice with each other but not with the game master.

The objective was somewhat similar to the Teamwork Tester—to find the pieces of the puzzle and insert them in the correct places. Each team had seventy-five minutes to complete as many puzzles as possible, receiving a certain number of points for each completed puzzle. The researchers had emphasized a role of communication in the process, suggesting that the choice of communication tools and ability to communicate to each other effectively had a significant impact on the teams' success.

Results and Interpretation of Teamwork Simulations

In both of the simulations, operators collect similar types of information. Teamwork Tester automatically records parameters such as start and completion time, number of movements needed to complete the puzzle, number of pieces that each player put in the correct position, and number of movements that each player performed. Based on this raw data, the simulation calculates a variety of metrics that can be interpreted to see how well each member performed on a personal level and how well the team as a whole completed the task (Figure 8.2). Team-level parameters include:

- **Team effectiveness** (based on the number of turns required to complete the puzzle)
- **Team speed** (based on the time required to complete the puzzle and number of team members)
- **Team leader** (individual who initiated the right pattern—other team members joined this individual in building the pattern he or she started)

On the individual level the simulation calculates the following parameters for each team member:

- **Effectiveness** (calculated as number of turns versus number of cubes completed by an individual)
- **Speed** (time spent on cubes rotations versus number of cubes completed by a learner)
- **Participation** (percentage of cubes completed by an individual, normalized by the number of members in the team)
- **Finishing work** (percentage of cubes that person operated and had finished)
- **Helping others** (percentage of cubes that person had finished helping another team member)
- **Disturbance** (percentage of cubes that person had "ruined," meaning that the cube was in the correct position before the person had touched it, and was left by this person in the incorrect position)
- **Impatience** (number of times the person pressed the "Done" button before the puzzle was really completed)

FIGURE 8.2

The parameters measured in the teamwork simulation described by O'Connell and coauthors were partly different from and partly similar to the Teamwork Tester simulation. We attribute the differences mostly to the variation in the scenarios. For example, as a part of efficiency, O'Connell and coauthors measured multiple "number of requests," such as the number of different requests to the game master. Because Teamwork Tester is automated and learners do not have to communicate with or request anything from a "game master," these parameters were absent in the Teamwork Tester scenario. At the same time, since the PanelPuzzle simulation involved verbal communications in different forms, authors could draw conclusions concerning the role of communications in collaboration and teamwork, while Teamwork Tester concentrates on nonverbal skills. Either way, the measurable results and useful data they produce go far beyond what one could draw from a corresponding activity in the physical world.

Virtual Worlds as a Teamwork Collaboration Tool

Various projects are increasingly performed by geographically dispersed teams, and this provides another possibility for using virtual worlds for the teamwork. In addition to being used as a tool for training and developing teamwork and leadership skills, virtual worlds are widely used as a platform for teamwork and collaborative activities by groups of people who are working at different physical locations. Members of these groups might have never met each other in person; they might live in different time zones, belong to different cultures, speak different languages, and sometimes even work in different organizations.

Unless we find a way to compensate for these differences, as well as for the lack of nonverbal cues, we might not be able to fully realize the potential of today's work environment. Teleconferencing and videoconferencing seem to be the most widely accepted tools for distance collaboration at the moment. It appears, however, that given equal access to videoconferencing and teleconferencing, few people go through the effort and expense to install and use videoconferencing in the corporate environment. Display-sharing software such as WebEX or GoToMeeting seem to have wider acceptance since they allow users to concentrate on the subject at hand, not facial features. At the same time, whenever there are more than four or five people on a call and unless all microphones except the speaker's are muted, it is close to impossible to recognize who is asking a question or commenting on a topic. If somebody starts a "sidebar" conversation (that might actually be quite important but not necessarily interesting or clear to everybody on the call), it can be the end of constructive conversation for all participants.

Second Life offers a compelling alternative to teleconferencing, videoconferencing, and display sharing software. Once logged in, users feel that they are participating in an event, not merely watching somebody else's presentation. The availability of slide presentations, streaming audio and video, whiteboards, mind mapping, and other tools allows participants to fully collaborate on any project. Many participants in Second Life collaboration sessions specifically mention the availability of multimodal communications (that is, simultaneous use of voice, text, and instant messages) as one of the benefits of using Second Life for collaboration (see Microsoft and Intel case studies, Chapter 6). There is also a degree of privacy, since participants can send private instant messages to other participants, as well as exchange text chat or speak by voice publicly.

Second Life provides another advantage in the form of the easy recording of text and audio conversations. Logs of all text exchanges and recorded audio and video can be used to simplify the creation of minutes for virtual meetings.

In the following sections we look at the characteristics of virtual teams and what kinds of leaders and management processes are necessary to help virtual teams complete a project effectively and efficiently.

Virtual Teams

Groups of employees who work together on a shared project from a distance using information and communications technologies (ICT) are known as "virtual teams." They can also be called "off-site teams," "off-site employees," "remote teams," "distance work," and "computer-supported cooperative work." Kirkman and Mathieu (2004) define virtual teams as "groups of workers with unique skills, who often reside in different geographical places and have to use for co-operation means of ICT in order to span the boundaries of time and space." While the use of electronic tools is a necessary part of the definition of virtual teams, it should be noted that most of the virtual teams' members do occasionally meet face-to-face. An increasing number of teams are using virtual worlds as their technology of choice in working collaboratively.

Kimball (1997) identified several different kinds of virtual teams, including:

- **Executive teams** (usually made up of managers with responsibilities for specific functions in the organization)
- **Project teams** (groups created around a specific task where members are selected for their expertise, and which generally function only for the life of the project)
- **Community of practice teams** (people working on common tasks or in the same professional field who voluntarily get together to share experiences and knowledge)

Virtual teams can link "islands of knowledge" into self-organizing, knowledge-sharing networks that foster collaboration and the spread of best practices. At the same time, this requires a new management mindset—breaking away from traditional command-and-control management of teams to a much looser management style that encourages cooperation and sharing of responsibilities among the team members.

Michael Schrage (1995) suggests that the concept of a team as an organizational structure with set roles may be outdated. He says, "The real basic structure of the workplace is the relationship. Each relationship is itself part of a larger network of relationships. These relationships can be measured along all kinds of dimensions—from political to professional expertise. The fact is that work gets done through these relationships." In light of this, virtual teams can be viewed as building blocks for organizational learning. Because virtual teams work at a distance, there's usually some kind of recording of the work of the team, which can be added to an organization's knowledge base.

As companies become more global and operate in dispersed geographic areas, virtual teams have become almost indispensable for businesses. The expertise needed to fulfill a company's mission can now be drawn from almost anywhere in the world. The existence of virtual teams generated new modes of communication, which have in turn influenced the way people work. For example, reliable asynchronous communications (e-mail, voice mail) allow team members to work different shifts in a continuous workflow.

The many benefits of virtual teams include less time needed to get the job done, reduced workspace costs, efficient product development, increased productivity, better customer service, better access to global markets, and benefits to the environment due to reduced travel (Horwitz et al. 2006). This means that "people can be recruited for their competencies, not just physical location" (Gould 2006). In many cases, physical disabilities become irrelevant because of an employee's ability to work from home in a virtual team. Also, in a virtual world, the fact that a person is represented by an avatar can mean that any disability or other physical characteristic remains hidden and is therefore not the source of discrimination or altered expectations.

Virtual teams add to business flexibility since they can adapt rapidly to changing circumstances. "Gaining competitive advantage in a global environment means continually reshaping the organization to maximize grants, address threats, and increase speed. The use of virtual teams has become a common way of doing this," contend Duarte and Snyder, in their 2007 book, *Mastering Virtual Teams*. "The goal is to leverage intellectual capital and apply it as quickly as possible."

Issues in Managing Virtual Teams

Gerda Mihhailova (2007) says that "turning ordinary teamwork fully (or at least partially) into virtual teamwork introduces a whole new range of problems for managers." Virtual teams can be "communication challenged, culturally challenged and task challenged" (Malhotra and Majchrzak

2005). Most of the problems don't come from the fact that virtual teams use technologies for maintaining contact but from the changing nature of the functioning of teams in the workplace. Teams are no longer fixed entities, drawn entirely from within an organization. Instead, employees may be part of several different teams, with members distributed throughout the organization and beyond, in varying geographical locations. Such teams may form and reform continuously, resulting in multiple reporting relationships for each team member.

We are just learning how to manage the complexity of virtual teams, so it is not surprising that a number of issues or problems can arise from these new forms of organizational collaboration. The 2004 review of the literature on virtual teams by Ann Powell and her colleagues revealed a number of issues that practitioners should be aware of in setting up and managing a virtual team. These issues include, among others:

▶ **Initial design and composition of the team.** Teams need to develop a shared language and a shared understanding of the team tasks. Team-building exercises, shared norms, and a clear team structure all contribute to the success of a virtual team.

▶ **Cultural differences among team members.** Cultural differences among team members can lead to coordination difficulties and create obstacles to effective communication.

▶ **Trust among team members.** Developing trust is a big issue in virtual teams as it is often hard to assess team members' trustworthiness if you have never met them. For many virtual teams, there is a need for trust to develop quickly. Interestingly, in virtual teams many members assume that the others are trustworthy unless there are indicators that they are not.

▶ **Coordination.** Coordination has been directly linked to virtual team performance, and the difficulties that virtual teams are facing in this area have been studied extensively. Coordination difficulties have been attributed to working across time zones, mixing of different cultures, and having members with different "mental models."

▶ **Team performance.** Most studies show little significant difference between the performance of virtual teams and face-to-face teams, although in one study, virtual teams generated more ideas than more traditional teams. On the other hand, virtual teams often take longer to reach a decision.

Leadership of Virtual Teams

DeRosa et al. (2004) say that for virtual teams "the lack of physical interaction results in reduced verbal, social, and status cues that are typically present in face-to-face (FTF) communication." This is because of the difficulty in creating a sense of "shared space" with the virtual teams. The negative impact of a lack of cues is lessened by the use of virtual worlds and avatars, which give much more context to team relationships compared to other electronic communications methods such as e-mail and instant messaging.

Leadership issues can arise, especially because many virtual teams are formed for short periods of time and can witness many changes in their membership. Virtual team managers need to learn new skills, including new ways to coordinate work, monitor employees, provide feedback, and resolve conflicts. For example, part of the shift from Web 1.0 to Web 2.0 technologies has been the change in emphasis from individual learning to team-based collaborative learning. This represents a fundamental shift in how learning takes place, as we move from a model of instructor-led teaching of individuals to one of learner-led finding, doing, and collaborating in small groups. Virtual world technology is on the leading edge of this shift.

Michael Fullan (2001), in his influential book *Leading in a Culture of Change*, states, "The more complex society gets, the more sophisticated leadership must become." Leadership in virtual worlds is not about traditional "command and control" structures but the provision of direction and support to team members when and where it is needed, as well as fostering the leadership of others. This is because problems in today's society have become so complex, and are constantly changing, that the old image of a "seasoned warrior" leading the troops into battle simply doesn't work anymore.

According to Fullan, true leadership has these five components: moral purpose, understanding change, relationship building, knowledge creation and sharing, and coherence making. In the end, a leader is the person who makes the best sense of a complex situation, helping a team to sort out what is happening, understand the context of an issue, and move in a specific direction to solve a problem.

Susan E. Kogler Hill (2007), writing on team leadership, identifies three important decisions that any leader must make: 1) Should I monitor the team or take action? 2) Should I intervene to meet task or relational needs? 3) Should I intervene internally or externally? She then enumerates the factors that make any team effective:

- A clear, elevating goal
- Results-driven structure
- Competent team members
- Unified commitment
- Collaborative climate
- Standards of excellence
- External support and recognition
- Principled leadership

What is meant by "principled leadership"? Peter Northouse (2007) thinks that ethical leaders "respect others," "serve others," "are just," "are honest," and "build community." These qualities apply to all team leaders—not just those in virtual worlds.

So what is different about leading teams in virtual worlds? That question is the subject of discussion in a very interesting "global outlook report" written in 2007 by IBM and Seriosity, Inc., titled "Virtual Worlds,

Real Leaders." The report argues that "leadership is as much a by-product of environment as it is intrinsic. Leadership happens quickly and easily in online games, often undertaken by otherwise reserved players, who surprise even themselves with their capabilities. There is no reason to think that the same cannot be done in corporate settings of various sizes, missions, and markets." (IBM and Seriosity 2007).

This doesn't mean that every person in an organization can or should lead, but finding the person who is the right leader at a particular time depends on the circumstances, the problem being faced, and the availability of human and other resources. In a fast-paced game or operation in a virtual world, leadership "emerges" as needed and is temporary, dissipating when the situation ends. This is a very different model of leadership from what we are accustomed to, but it is a necessary mental shift to make.

There are often many opportunities to lead within tasks in a virtual world, whether it is a game or a simulation. The IBM/Seriosity report states, "Spreading around the leadership wealth in this way provides the opportunity for many players to try on leadership roles, decide if leadership agrees with them, and pursue it further if so inclined. Also, there is no expectation of permanence in these leadership roles, an important factor that encourages experimentation."

Clearly, there is a lot that traditional organizations can learn about team processes and leadership by having employees interact in virtual worlds.

 ## Conclusions and Best Practices

The following best practices should be kept in mind for teamwork and leadership training in virtual worlds:

► Virtual worlds provide an efficient platform for teamwork building and leadership development activities.

▶ Observations of teamwork and leadership exercises are important. However, to reap real benefits of using virtual worlds, use simulations that record trainee actions and provide you with objective data in addition to observations. Save raw, unprocessed data that were recorded during the simulation. If you decide to change parameters or process data differently, using other metrics, statistical analyses, or software, you can always do it later using raw data.

▶ Use an outside database for data storage and a Web interface for reviewing results.

▶ Use to the fullest the technological advantages of virtual worlds such as:
  –the ability to create mind maps and charts as a result of a brainstorming meeting
  –the ability to demonstrate and alter 3-D models
  –the ability to record/produce minutes of virtual meetings

▶ Encourage your employees to try out leadership roles in the nonthreatening environment of the virtual world.

Doing It Asynchronously: Training Simulations in Second Life

In previous chapters we have generally been discussing *synchronous training*. This is a type of training where instructor and trainees have to be present together in the location where the training takes place, whether in real life or in a virtual world. Most often, this is a classroom-type event, a meeting, or a teamwork activity that requires all the learners to be present and work on a task at the same time. The perceived necessity to conduct training in a synchronous mode, with an instructor leading the training at all times, limits the basic appeal of training in virtual worlds.

> "What happens if a big asteroid hits Earth? Judging from realistic simulations involving a sledge hammer and a common laboratory frog, we can assume it will be pretty bad."
>
> —*Dave Barry, bestselling American author and Pulitzer Prize–winning humorist*

Indeed, when employing electronic-based learning ("e-learning"), we expect trainees to be able to learn and practice on their own and the instructor to serve as a resource and a safety net. "Anytime and anywhere" has been written on the banners of the e-learning revolution since it began. However, are you ready to staff your virtual world project 24/7? Not likely. And that's OK.

For each disadvantage, Second Life and other virtual worlds have an overriding advantage. Although the inability to conduct training asynchronously is still a limitation in some virtual worlds, advanced virtual worlds such as Second Life allow you to create asynchronous training modules and seamlessly blend these modules into existing e-learning programs.

However, not all e-learning modules are well suited for implementation in virtual worlds. Materials dealing with descriptive knowledge, and therefore requiring processing and remembering significant amounts of text, audio, and video, would be better left as Web-based e-learning units. On the other hand, training modules that involve acquiring and practicing new skills, collaboration and communication with others, or procedural knowledge are better taught in a virtual world. Synchronous training has a role here, but to make training more efficient you will certainly want to use training simulations. Training simulations are especially important in cases when real-life training requires real working equipment, can be dangerous, or is expensive.

"Simulation" is an interesting term: everybody seems to know what it is; however, when you search the literature trying to find a precise definition, you run into conflicting, and sometimes opposing, definitions. The meanings range from a "formal mathematical or computer model constructed to predict behavior of a certain physical system" (Prensky 2001), to "creating a model of natural systems, including human systems, in order to gain insight into their functioning" (Aldrich 2003), to "interactions between people, such as role-playing" (Jones 1985). Manninen (2002) stated that "simulations are representations of the real-world systems that are flexible and variable to a degree that allows them to evolve." We would agree with this last definition with one exception: the most important feature of a training simulation is not visual resemblance to a real-world system but its functionality—our ability to use it to teach and learn skills that are applicable in the real world. We therefore define a "training simulation" as a representation of a device or a process that is flexible and variable to the degree that it allows a user to learn essential skills applicable to professional activities and life in the real world.

Crookall et al. (1987) think the difference between simulations and games is that games are purely fictional worlds and do not intend to represent any real-world system. From our perspective, this distinction is superficial. As long as a learner acquires skills that he or she will use in real life through interaction with a situation that requires the practice of these skills, we are talking about a training simulation. For example, an obstacle course can be a training simulation when a group of students uses it to learn teamwork and leadership skills. The same obstacle course can be a game when a person using it tries to get from start to finish purely for entertainment.

We can divide all training simulations into two groups:

1. Simulations where a user learns new skills by interacting with an object. Let us call them person-to-object, or PTO, simulations.
2. Simulations where a user learns new skills by interacting with other people. Let us call them person-to-person, or PTP, simulations.

 ## Person-to-Object Simulations

PTO simulations work best in three types of scenarios:

- ► Procedural knowledge training
- ► Equipment training
- ► Three-dimensional visualization

Procedural Training

Even though procedural training is often associated with medicine, it can be used and, indeed, is used in practically all industries. Procedural training is simply learning correct procedures and processes for performing a given task. You do not have to operate any equipment to have a procedure in place. A script for routing a tech support call to the correct person is just as much a procedure as is a sequence of steps for taking blood for analysis. If the procedures fundamental to your business are not codified and taught, productivity will eventually suffer, as employees are forced to either improvise a new procedure on the spot or spend time trying to locate the last person known to have used a tested procedure.

Procedural knowledge in many cases gives a company a unique competitive advantage. Codifying this knowledge is the first step toward formalizing the best practices you employ in the business. In some situations, such as emergency response, "procedure" must become the "second nature" of a trainee. In others, while not as critical, it must be practiced until it is performed flawlessly. By formalizing procedural training, you assess and quantify employees' understanding of the best practices for their jobs. They will become more confident, efficient, and motivated and will make fewer mistakes as they learn the correct procedures.

Training should also include simulations that encourage learners to apply their newly acquired knowledge. This way you can both verify that a procedure is remembered (becoming part of passive memory) and can be used correctly (becoming part of active memory). Using simulations is very beneficial in complex training situations, especially those that involve multiple decision points followed by branching paths that lead to dissimilar outcomes. Using simulations in virtual worlds helps learners experience complex situations in a safe and controlled environment. Any organization will benefit from making staff training in operational procedures more efficient. Employees in any industry, from insurance adjusters processing claims to machinists undergoing safety and emergency training to city police learning response procedures to welders in the Occupational Health and Safety Association (OSHA) training, can benefit from procedural training in virtual worlds.

In many cases, virtual tools do not allow you to create a precise model of every aspect of a piece of equipment. However, a virtual world provides unlimited opportunities and a great environment for efficient learning of procedural steps, sequences of actions, and making decisions. It would take significant effort, for example, to build an exact model of a factory floor in Second Life. However, if the purpose is to train employees in the ordered steps of what should be done in case of an electrical fire, you do not need high-fidelity models of all the machinery installed in the factory. Rough sketches of equipment will suffice, as long as your model includes a floor plan made to scale with the locations of emergency shut-off buttons, telephones, carbon dioxide fire extinguishers, and emergency exits. Making accurate models of this relevant equipment would be helpful for learning.

Chapter 10 provides a case study of an excellent example of how Second Life was used for procedural knowledge training. The University of Kansas Medical Center created and successfully used an operating room simulation in Second Life for teaching anesthesia procedures to nurses. Among other beneficial outcomes, this implementation of Second Life for procedural training demonstrated that separating physical details ("how to") and process details ("why and in what order") reduces cognitive load and improves overall results. Because the platform provided an opportunity to accurately and realistically model the operating environment and equipment, trainees subconsciously learned other important facets of the situation, such as the location of equipment and materials, even though these topics were not explicitly taught.

Equipment Training

Because the complexities of modern equipment and its costs are increasing, the requirements for training employees to operate equipment often include lowering the training costs and decreasing training time while maintaining high standards of quality and safety.

To meet these requirements, many instructional designers turned their attention to virtual worlds, and equipment training was one of the first areas to attract their attention. Until recently, technical difficulties in creating realistic models of machinery, as well as a lack of software specialists familiar with Second Life programming, prevented many interesting ideas from being implemented. It appears, however, that the situation is changing. For example, British Petroleum (BP) has recently created a Second Life model of a typical BP gas station complete with tanks and pipe systems for employee training.

Employees learn about equipment and procedures in a safe environment and can see the effect of actions they take. "Trainees could 'see' underground and observe the effect of using safety devices to control the flow of gasoline. They were able to observe the workings of a very complex system in a way they could never have done in real life" (Galagan 2008).

Equipment training does not need to be only within a company. Manufacturers of complex equipment realize that training their customers in operating and maintaining that equipment is often a significant part of the price they have to charge. For each piece of machinery a company sells, it may have to fly in several technicians from a client company and train them for a number of days in its training facility. If the creation of local technical support centers is not feasible, service personnel also have to be flown to customer locations around the world on a regular basis. In such situations, equipment training in virtual worlds becomes very practical.

Even moving parts of equipment training classes into a virtual world, and supplementing them with self-study units where learners can go over certain modules and refresh their knowledge, greatly reduces training costs and therefore makes a product more competitive. Offering virtual world technical support along with the training, where a technician can show a client what needs to be done on a model of the equipment rather than trying to explain it over the phone, reduces costs while cutting response time and increases customer satisfaction.

Three-Dimensional Visualization

Since early humans started representing the three-dimensional (3-D) world as two-dimensional (2-D) paintings on the walls of caves, most visualizations that people have created have been two-dimensional. The work of creating 3-D reality never stopped, however, starting from ancient sculptures and the invention of linear perspective in the fourteenth century and leading to today's three-dimensional movies and computer software. Second Life provides a relatively easy way to create 3-D models—from models of the human body used to teach anatomy to 3-D models of industrial machinery that allow compliance training or the teaching of OSHA lockout/tagout procedures. (These are Occupational Safety and Health Administration requirements on what to do and how to do it safely if a machine breaks and needs to be repaired.)

There are two ways to create something in 3-D in Second Life. The first approach is to build an object using simple "prims," or primitive objects such as spheres, cubes, cylinders, or cones. You can combine multiple prims into a complex model. However, when the object you want to model contains surfaces with complex shapes, such as a car fender or a human heart, it is close to impossible to create a realistic model using only simple geometric objects. To build accurate objects with complex geometry, you need to use sculptured prims (see Chapter 5 for more details).

Adding scripts to 3-D models allows you to program special behaviors into an object, increasing its value for 3-D visualization. For example, you can program a model of a human heart to move as if it were pumping blood when a learner touches (clicks with a mouse) a certain part of the model. You can also add sound to the visualization, asking a learner to distinguish between healthy sounds and those that might be specific to a particular heart ailment. Such three-dimensional models are a great help for geographically dispersed teams collaborating on the development of a new product or a sales team doing a remote presentation to a prospect.

 ## Person-to-Person Simulations

PTP simulations, or role-plays, are perhaps the most common type of simulations used in the real world. Not surprisingly, these were also the first simulations tried in virtual worlds. Communications and all its application-specific variations, such as sales, recruiting, cultural training, and dealing with difficult people, were the first areas of corporate training tested in virtual worlds simply because of their innate interactivity.

The apparent ease of transferring a role-play from a classroom to a virtual classroom was an important factor as well. But, synchronous role-play programs that mimic existing training, however detailed and elaborate, only scratch the surface of the capabilities of virtual worlds in the area of communications training. No doubt, synchronous role-play exercises in virtual worlds do work and are beneficial for corporate training. They eliminate travel, save time, and help reduce the reluctance of some adult learners to participate in role-playing. Today, however, we can go well beyond synchronous role-playing by creating *asynchronous* simulations using *robotic avatars* in programmable 3-D virtual worlds.

Asynchronous Person-to-Robot Simulations

In a virtual world you are represented by an avatar—"a computer user's representation of himself or herself . . . in the form of a three-dimensional model"—as Wikipedia explains the term. Your avatar is your alter ego in the virtual world. It can do plenty of things that you perhaps cannot: fly, teleport, look thirty years younger and fifty pounds slimmer. One thing your avatar cannot do is have its own free will. If it flies, it does so only because you command it to fly. If it says something, it is only because you say something. If it looks a bit slimmer, it is only because you made it so.

Second Life enthusiasts have created a set of programming libraries that allow a competent software engineer to create a computer program to operate an avatar, or what we call a "robotic avatar." This is an avatar that is not under direct human control but is controlled by a computer program. There are obvious benefits to being the magician behind the curtain, but there is also a detriment—you do not want to spend all of your waking hours behind a computer controlling your avatar. The robotic avatar attempts to rectify this. He (or she, or it—we can even bring to life the Scarecrow or the Cowardly Lion here) does not need a human being operating behind the scenes. A robotic avatar is operated by computer software, and the only way you can influence its behavior is indirectly, through changes to the program and/or the database it uses. In fact, it is a good practice to keep all information about a robot's behavior, the whole branching tree of possible paths of action, in a database. A program will then access the database when it needs to find out what the robot is supposed to do next. The robot's database can be located on any Internet-connected computer network *outside* Second Life. Most users prefer to put it on their company's network, behind the enterprise's firewall. In this configuration, your intellectual property and other proprietary information are kept outside Second Life, in the same secure environment as other sensitive information on your network.

THE TURING TEST

There are few philosophical papers that are quoted more frequently than Alan Turing's *Computing Machinery and Intelligence* (Turing 1950). The paper discusses many aspects of computations and artificial intelligence, but the most famous and the most quoted element of it is the "Test." Turing describes an imitation game, in which a human simultaneously interrogates another human and a computer. The interrogator does not know who is carrying the conversation on the other end: a human or a computer. Turing suggests that if the interrogator could not distinguish the human from the machine by questioning alone, we could reasonably say that the computer possesses intelligence. The Test changed the direction of many scientific and philosophical discussions. By proposing a seemingly simple test, Turing managed to avoid fruitless but intense philosophical and religious discussions of consciousness and get to the very root of the question. The proposed "imitation game" is now commonly called "The Turing Test" or "The Turing Test for Intelligence."

Robotic Avatars vs. Artificial Intelligence

A word of caution is in order: when we are speaking about robotic avatars, we are not talking about a sophisticated level of artificial intelligence. This is not a case of having a bunch of inexpensive, no-maintenance virtual instructors ready to teach any and all subjects around the clock. The level of artificial intelligence today, and perhaps for some years ahead, will not provide you with a tool you can readily use in business. The sidebar that follows provides an example of one of the author's dialogues with A.L.I.C.E. (Artificial Linguistic Internet Computer Entity), an award-winning natural language artificial intelligence chat robot (you can chat with her at http://alice.pandorabots.com).

DIALOGUE WITH ARTIFICIAL INTELLIGENCE

Human: Hi

  ALICE: Hello there.

Human: What's new?

  ALICE: Not much. What's new with you?

Human: I became interested in artificial intelligence.

  ALICE: What happened after that?

Human: I stopped by to talk to you.

  ALICE: You are not the boss of me.

Human: Granted, but what do you think about artificial intelligence?

  ALICE: I've been waiting for you.

Human: Some people say that you are an example of AI.

  ALICE: Interesting observation.

Human: Are you?

  ALICE: I won't say yes or no right now.

Human: Why not?

  ALICE: Ambiguous: sure, or the explanation is rather complicated.

Human: What do you know about Second Life?

  ALICE: Have you tried another program?

Human: Yes, I did.

ALICE: Ahem. Have you tried another program? You did?

Human: Yes.

ALICE: Er.

Human: You didn't answer my question: what do you know about Second Life?

ALICE: Please help me improve my communication skills. What would have been an appropriate response?

Human: You could say yes or no or you could ask me, "What is Second Life?"

ALICE: No or you could ask me what is Second Life.

Human: OK, what do you think about training in the corporate world?

ALICE: Let me think about it. Great.

Human: You think it's great?

ALICE: Signs point to yes. Ask Dancing Alice if it is.

Human: What is especially attractive to you?

ALICE: That's an interesting question. I'll come back to that in a minute.

Human: It sounds like you try to avoid answering direct questions.

ALICE: Interesting gossip: unknown person said I try to avoid answering direct questions.

Human: My name is Alex Heiphetz.

ALICE: Hey Alex Heiphetz. What did you mean by it? That is interesting gossip: unknown person said I try to avoid answering direct questions.

Human: Why don't you answer my question?

ALICE: I love talking to people about that. My botmaster has programmed me with more than replies.

After reading this dialogue, you will probably agree that at this stage it is premature to discuss business applications based on robots driven by artificial intelligence. Nevertheless, robotic avatars are something you should investigate even though they do not use artificial intelligence. Instead of trying to create a generalized robot that would be able to carry on intelligent conversations in any area, robotic avatars can be used as virtual agents in branching story simulations.

A branching story is a simulation genre where a trainee is given background information on a situation and then proceeds to complete a task by making choices at different points in the process. In other words, user decisions determine the flow of events. This approach may be less glamorous than using artificial intelligence, but it works very well in training, providing learners with a guiding framework. Branching story simulations are widely used in corporate training, and prior to their use in virtual worlds employed Flash, streaming video, and other on-screen methods of story visualization. Moving branching story simulations to virtual worlds is a step forward compared with 2-D on-screen visualization methods, since virtual worlds provide a more realistic, immersive environment that is second only to personal experience in real life. At the same time, the cost of creating branching story simulations in virtual worlds is lower than creating a similar simulation using other methods.

Sometimes, simulations can include only robots "playing out" a realistic situation. For example, we recently discussed creating a training simulation for a medical school. One of the ideas on the table was creating a robot-to-robot simulation, such as a robot-physician examining and talking to a robot-patient. The student's role in the simulation would be to observe how the robot-physician is working with the robot-patient and to write a report on the correct and incorrect actions, an accurate or inaccurate diagnosis, and the course of treatment proposed by the "physician."

Communication Simulations in Second Life: How Do They Work?

Let's review the creation and deployment of a simple communications simulation using the branching story method. The simulation for the purpose of this analysis is highly simplified so that we can fully concentrate on the principles and procedures behind the creation and rolling out of a simulation in Second Life.

IN SECOND LIFE. In order to use a simulation in Second Life, a trainee logs in and teleports to the simulation location. Once he or she presses the button to start the simulation, the scenario begins to unfold. One or more robotic avatars appear on the scene (depending on the setup, the robotic avatar can be a secretary, doctor, manager, customer, coworker, etc.) and starts a conversation. At a certain point the trainee sees a dialogue box and can select the best response out of several available choices (Figure 9.1). The robotic avatar responds (by text or by voice, or both), and the trainee makes the next selection.

FIGURE 9.1

This process continues until the simulation either ends successfully or is interrupted due to incorrect choices made by the trainee. As the simulation progresses, additional robotic avatars can appear in the scene. For example, a salesperson in training might have to talk to several employees at different levels of the organization in order to set up an appointment or talk to a decision maker.

Once the simulation is completed, the trainee receives immediate feedback through a Second Life pop-up window with a link to a Web page displaying the simulation results. Typically, the results will include a score as well as a detailed analysis of each step and explanations on what the trainee did well or what mistakes he or she made (Figure 9.2). After reviewing the results, a trainee can repeat the simulation and select a different set of choices.

COMMUNICATION / SALES TRAINING RESULTS

Your score is 50 out of 120.

Your opening was very good. You addressed doctor's concerns about product A and that gave you a good start.

You managed well to take few more minutes of doctor's time to present product B.

However, failure to address doctor's concerns about side effects of product B ended your meeting. before you had a chance to introduce product C. You managed well to take few more minutes of doctor's time to present product B. However, failure to address doctor's concerns about side effects of product B ended your meeting before you had a chance to introduce product C. You managed well to take few more minutes of doctor's time to present product B. However, failure to address doctor's concerns about side effects of product B ended your meeting before you had a chance to introduce product C. You managed well to take few more minutes of doctor's time to present product B. However, failure to address doctor's concerns about side effects of product B ended your meeting before you had a chance to introduce product C. You managed well to take few more minutes of doctor's time to present product B. However, failure to address doctor's concerns about side effects of product B ended your meeting before you had a chance to introduce product C.

Please, try simulation again with the different choices.

Your dialog is below:

Doctor: Hey, how is it going? It is another crazy day here. What is new?

You: Last time I was here you expressed some concern about product A. I have this information for you, and I also want to talk about products B and C.

Doctor: Great, I am glad you remember that question about product A. You know, a lot of reps that call on me just say the same thing every time they come in. But look, I only have a few minutes and that sounds like a lot to cover. Let's get started, and I will let you know when I run out of time.

You: In closing, let me remind you that product A is on 90% of the local formularies, which I am sure your patients will appreciate. Can I get your commitment to continue precscribing product A?

Doctor: Well, that's fine that product A is on formularies, but I do not prescribe a drug just because it is on formulary. I prescribe it because it is safe and effective for my patients. You said you have other things to talk to me about, so let's move on.

You: Yes, I understand, but will you still prescribe product B for your patients?

Doctor: Well, I would like to have my concerns about side effects addressed before I start prescribing it. I want to make sure it is safe. Now, sorry but I ran out of time. Thank you for stopping by.

FIGURE 9.2

BEHIND THE SCENES. Behind any branching story simulation there is a flowchart that shows the simulation paths and decision points. Figure 9.3 illustrates this using an example of a very simple simulation. The setup is straightforward: the trainee, playing the role of a salesperson, enters the office of a prospect and talks to a receptionist. Here is how the simulation unfolds:

▶ After an initial greeting, the gatekeeper asks the trainee to state the purpose of her visit.

▶ The trainee has three choices of how to respond:
  1. Introduce herself and tell the receptionist that she has an appointment with purchasing manager Mr. Smith
  2. Introduce herself and tell the receptionist that she is there to see purchasing manager Mr. Smith
  3. Tell the receptionist that she is there to see a purchasing manager responsible for the purchase of the printing services

▶ Depending on the trainee's response the receptionist either (1) verifies that Mr. Smith is expecting the visitor and welcomes the trainee in, or (2) asks if she has an appointment, or (3) tells her that all the purchasing managers are busy but she is welcome to leave her sales materials and the receptionist will be sure to pass them to the correct person. Obviously case (1) is the best outcome, while case (3) is the worst.

Even for a simple simulation it is a good idea to create a branching story diagram similar to the one shown in Figure 9.3 to visualize the logic of the simulation. For complex real-life simulations, creating a branching story diagram(s) is critical.

For this scenario, the branching story chart looks simple. However, it quickly becomes increasingly complex as multiple decision points and possible paths are added, as required in real-life complex simulations. Instructional designers are probably familiar with the situation in which they have to submit complex written specifications to Flash developers to

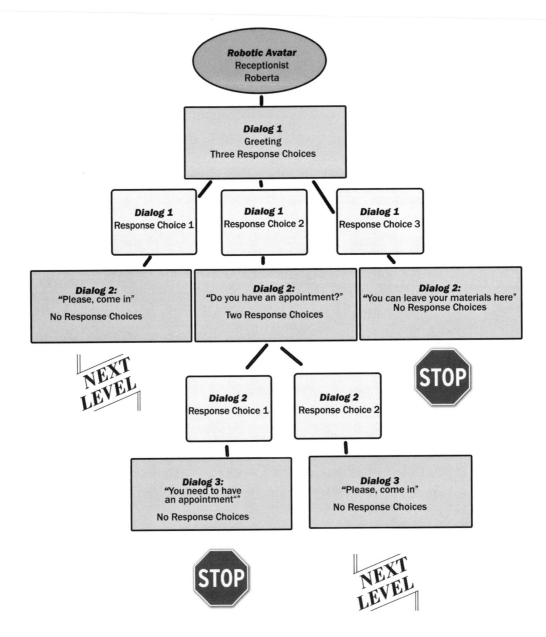

FIGURE 9.3

be hard-coded into the simulation. The process of developing specifications consumes a significant portion of development time and budget. Even more so, if you want to change anything based on trainees' feedback after receiving the completed product (as you often do), you have to go through the same process again.

The good news is that Second Life provides an easy way to develop, control, and modify simulations. Even better, some vendors have started to provide software that allows you to create and edit branching stories behind simulations via a Web-based graphical user interface without writing a single line of computer code. As a result, instructional designers generally do not have to involve computer programmers to create a simulation or to modify it later. Building simulations with this kind of software boils down to building a branching story diagram using a graphical interface similar to what you would find in traditional flowchart software (Figure 9.4).

With this approach, you create the flow of a simulation by dragging containers with characters, dialogues, responses, and actions; you then position them on the screen and connect them with arrows. Clicking on each container opens context-sensitive dialogue where you enter (or edit) all relevant information—dialogue text, response text, score and assessment for each response, and selected gestures and actions that the robotic avatar should perform (Figures 9.5, 9.6, and 9.7). Once a simulation is created and saved, it is available for trainees in Second Life. The same graphical interface is used to edit any part of the simulation once it has been created.

As we have mentioned, the server that runs the simulation is located on your enterprise network, outside Second Life. When the user runs the simulation, all sensitive data such as trainee information and results of the exercises are also routed to the database behind your corporate firewall. The data is accessible to the administrator via a password-protected Web interface. No sensitive information is stored on Second Life servers, adding an additional layer of security to your Second Life training program.

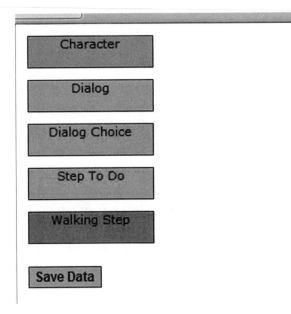

FIGURE 9.4

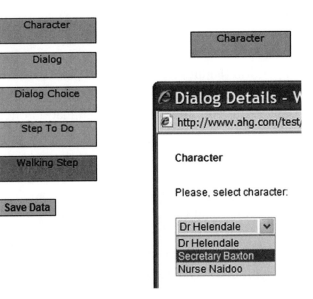

FIGURE 9.5

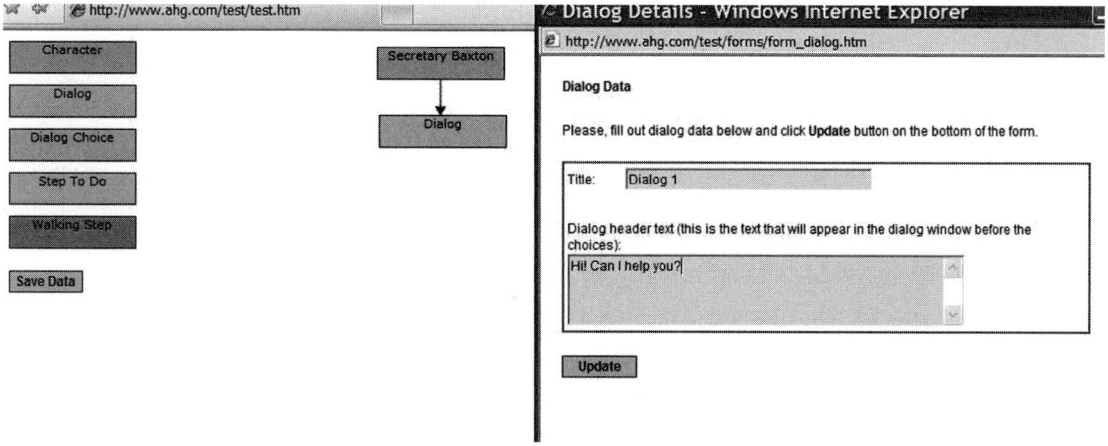

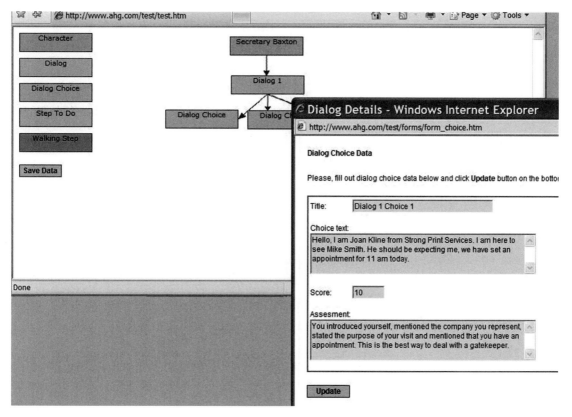

FIGURE 9.6

FIGURE 9.7

Saving and Retrieving Simulation Data

In order to be useful, all types of simulations must have some form of feedback that tells the learner what was done correctly and what requires further improvement. For virtual worlds, it means that in order to create an asynchronous training simulation you need the ability to program objects to react to the learner's actions, provide textual/audio/video comments, and record the learner's actions for processing and review. Second Life has built-in tools for this task—scripts attached to objects.

In other virtual worlds you will need to use an application programming interface (API) to perform this task. Using an API generally requires more programming skills and effort than writing scripts for simulations in Second Life. Because there is no way to keep data within Second Life or other virtual worlds, it is a good practice in implementing training simulations to include a connection to an outside database or a learning management system (LMS).

Whether you choose to store the data in the LMS or in a stand-alone database depends on the particular situation. In either case, the data should be accessible via a graphical interface that provides an easy way to do at least some of the following:

▶ Provide administrators with easy tools for access control and the ability to create lists of users (with their avatar names) who are allowed to run the simulation.

▶ Provide administrators with the ability to control variable simulation parameters (for example, the amount of time users are allowed to spend working on the simulation, or the number of unsuccessful attempts a user is allowed during any single session).

▶ Provide learners with controlled access to registration and information about the simulation.

▶ Provide both administrator(s) and learners with scheduling features, including the ability to find the first available time slot, or all available time slots, within a certain period and the ability to reserve a time slot for a specific user or group of users in the case of a team simulation.

▶ Provide both administrator(s) and users with the ability to review the results. Of course, users should be able to access only their own results. Instructors will have the ability to view all the results, as well as statistics and reports on how many learners ran the simulation, how many attempts they needed on average to get a passing grade, the average time required to complete the task, and other relevant data for a specific trainee and a group as a whole.

Virtual Worlds vs. the Web: Much in Common, Lots of Differences

Because we are talking about connecting virtual worlds and the World Wide Web, this would be a good place to discuss their capabilities in more general terms, especially because we often hear that virtual worlds are described as "Web 3.0." Even though virtual worlds are hosted on the servers that are connected to networks and may be accessible from the Internet, describing them as "Web 3.0" or the "three-dimensional Internet" or "3-D Web" is an oversimplification and is misleading from a usability standpoint.

While using these terms to describe virtual worlds might be good enough from a purely technical standpoint, qualitative differences make them very different in terms of how and why we use them. From the very beginning, the World Wide Web was about searching for, sharing, and receiving information. Information can come in different forms; it started with text (few people remember, but there were browsers for the Unix platform that could not display anything but text) and then, step-by-step, images, sounds, voice, video, movies, and animations were added to the Web. When users did not have the capability to display information in their browser, they could download many types of files to their computers and use additional software to open and work with these files.

The development of Web 2.0 was an essential step toward increased interactivity. According to Wikipedia, Web 2.0 refers to a "second generation of Web development and design, which facilitates communication, secure information sharing, interoperability, and collaboration on the World Wide Web. Web 2.0 concepts have led to the development and evolution of Web-based communities, hosted services, and applications; such as social-networking sites, video-sharing sites, wikis, blogs, and folksonomies." According to Paul Graham's essay (Graham 2005) and the Wikipedia article on Web 2.0 (Ibid.), the term was coined by Dale Dougherty and Craig Cline and became widely known after the O'Reilly Media Web 2.0 conference in 2004.

The concept is sometimes hard to understand, because there is no single technical or software development to which one could point to as the beginning or foundation of Web 2.0. Rather, as users gradually changed the ways they integrated the Web into their everyday work and leisure, new tools appeared to accommodate closer and deeper social and collaborative interactions on the Web. The "guest books" of the early Web expanded their functionality and became "Web logs," or "blogs," and, later, "microblogs." The "FAQ" (or Frequently Asked Questions) sections of the websites acquired the ability to be created and edited by groups of users who were not necessarily the administrators of that website and became "wikipedias," or "wikis" (the best known example of this is Wikipedia).

Web 2.0 sites allow users to do much more than to search for and retrieve the information. New applications allow users to truly collaborate on creating content, new information, and new knowledge. The more people use these applications, the higher is their effectiveness and benefits to each user and to all users as a group (think eBay, Wikipedia, Craigslist, and Skype as examples). In spite of all the differences between Web 1.0 and Web 2.0 (and some suggest that these differences are quantitative rather than qualitative), the indisputable fact is that they are rooted in the need to share data in one form or another.

Virtual worlds replace simple networking and interactivity with shared experience, experiential learning, and collaboration. The difference is fundamental to such a degree that methods that work equally well in Web 1.0 *and* Web 2.0 are useless or even counterproductive in a virtual world. A good example of this ineffectiveness would be a text document. Text documents, in the form of a simple text or with hypertext language "markups" are the foundation of both Web 1.0 and Web 2.0. In a virtual world, however, text is hard to deal with and sometimes is almost impossible to read. The Second Life platform provides no additional benefits to using text outside the very limited areas of signs, pointers, and short informational note cards. The latter are read in a separate window of a virtual world program, just as you would read a short note in a text editor. Try putting lecture notes, a course outline, or a promotional brochure in a virtual world and the first question you will hear would be "Why? Why do we have to go through the trouble of connecting to the virtual world to access something that we could see much more conveniently in a Web browser?"

Information search in Second Life is another bottleneck that is currently light years behind Yahoo! or Google. Perhaps in the (not-too-distant) future search engines will be capable of indexing and locating information across the different virtual worlds just as easily as they do today with websites. But today it is not anywhere close. In fact, the most reliable way to find something specific in Second Life or any other virtual world is to do a Web search. With any luck, you will find an event or object you are looking for and it will be accompanied by direct link to a Second Life location, known as SLURL. Conversely, if you want others to be able to locate you in a virtual world, do not discount the importance of placing direct links to your virtual world project on your website.

The situation is the opposite for experiential learning and collaboration. Numerous case studies and research (Massey and Montoya 2008; Massey et al. 2009; Social Science Research Institute 2008; TechRadar 2008) suggest that experiential and collaborative learning is far more effective in virtual worlds. As a result, we do not see virtual worlds fully replacing Web-based training. Instead, it is wise to choose tools and platforms that are most appropriate for the task at hand: virtual worlds for experiential and procedural learning and collaboration, and the Web for descriptive learning and information search and exchange.

 ## Conclusions and Best Practices

Because delivery mechanisms for virtual worlds and Web-based training address different aspects of the learning cycle, they work best together in producing a coherent training program. Use virtual worlds for experiential training and the Web for descriptive training, as well as for accessing and handling results of virtual world modules. Making detailed reports on specific tasks and overall progress reports available to both trainee and instructor expedites learning and increases the ROI of the training program.

In a learning program such as communications, sales, leadership, or diversity training that deals with interaction between people, robots can be very useful as a part of a self-study unit. During an initial session, the instructor helps trainees to outline the task and sets up benchmarks and requirements. After an orientation lesson led by an instructor—which can be held in class, as a webinar, or in Second Life—trainees can log in and run the simulation as many times as they need to in order to become comfortable with their assignment.

Various research studies (for example, see Murphy et al. 1997) show that 60 to 90 percent of information that a person receives during communication comes from nonverbal cues. Second Life simulations greatly benefit from usage of animated gestures and sounds that correspond closely to body language, facial expressions, and sounds in real life. Providing appropriate nonverbal cues along with verbal response allows you to create immersive simulations. This makes Second Life training systems uniquely fit for "soft skills" training.

Procedural Training in Second Life: University of Kansas Medical Center Case Study

quite often, people outside the training business think of a "procedure" as something that happens in a hospital, or while operating special equipment. While of course procedures are used in any type of business, it is not surprising that one of the most innovative cases of procedural training comes from a medical school.

> "The history of liberty has largely been the history of the observance of procedural safeguards."
> —*Felix Frankfurter, American jurist, 1882–1965*

A large part of nursing education involves training students in the many necessary processes and procedures. The Nurse Anesthesia (NURA) department of the University of Kansas Medical Center (KUMC) has been successfully teaching online courses—and constantly seeking to improve training—for more than ten years. When KUMC started using Second Life for communication and presentations, NURA immediately recognized the potential of the new platform and proposed the idea of using it for the nursing training.

A team led by David M. Antonacci and Stephanie P. Gerald of KUMC Teaching & Learning Technologies (TLT) department supported the technical side of the project. After debating the widest educational possibilities versus the most realistic project scope, the two departments decided to start with a virtual world operating-room simulation, using Second Life simulation capabilities to help first-year NURA students learn a basic induction procedure.

Induction is a complex medical procedure in which a nurse anesthetist prepares a patient for surgery. It starts with the hospital staff rolling the patient into the operating room, where the nurse anesthetist attaches a variety of medical devices to the patient and ultimately administers an induction agent to anesthetize the patient for surgery. Induction involves approximately thirty major steps, with numerous decision points often branching into additional sub-procedures depending on the patient's condition and response to treatment.

During training, students must learn the sequence of steps involved in the induction procedure, and the simulation helps them to do this in a safe and controlled learning space. It does not provide students with tactile feedback and is not intended to teach them how to manipulate actual physical equipment or patients. These skills are better taught in the physical world, using real equipment. Rather, it's the *sequence of events* that is at issue in the simulated training. For example, students learn *when* to use a laryngoscope in the induction procedure using simulation, but they learn *how* to use the laryngoscope for intubation later, using a real laryngoscope and a mannequin-like patient simulator.

Even though the virtual world does not provide practice with the physical "how-to" aspects of induction, the immersive setting does allow students to learn the sequence of steps and branching decision making—which, when it comes to anesthesia, is as important as the physical aspects. Separating these functions reduces cognitive load for the nurse in training and improves the overall result by breaking a very complex procedure into manageable units. In other words, students master execution of the induction routine using the virtual world simulation. By the time they advance to the next level, they are able to concentrate fully on learning how to physically handle the patient and equipment without being distracted by trying to learn the sequence of steps.

 ## Simulation of Induction Procedure

The virtual world simulation begins when a student moves his or her avatar into the virtual operating room, which is an accurate reproduction of a KUMC hospital operating room (Figure 10.1). To build the simulation, TLT met with NURA faculty in a real operating room, and staff took pictures of equipment as the NURA faculty described and demonstrated the induction process. These pictures were used both as models to build needed virtual equipment and as textures, or surfaces, for this equipment (Figure 10.2). The ability to use images as textures in Second Life greatly reduced the time needed to build complex objects and created an almost lifelike reproduction of the operating room. (Fringe benefit: because the operating room is modeled accurately and realistically, the project led to an unanticipated outcome—students subconsciously learned the location of equipment in the real operating room.)

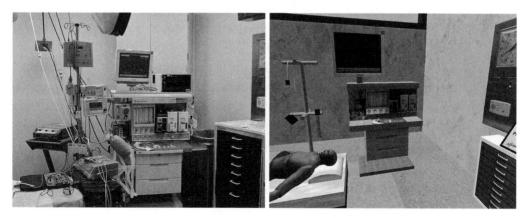

FIGURE 10.1

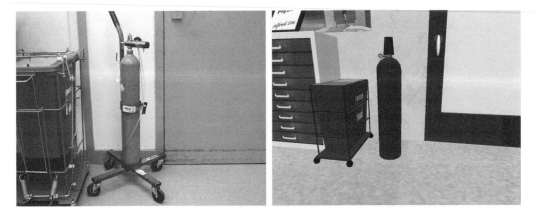

FIGURE 10.2

After entering the virtual world operating room, the student clicks a large object, called the main controller, to start the simulation. The main controller records the avatar's name and begins communicating with the other objects and equipment in the operating room. The student then works through the induction process by clicking on equipment objects in the sequence appropriate for the procedure. When clicked, the equipment attaches itself to the virtual patient (a human-shaped object, not an avatar). Depending on which piece of equipment was clicked, other objects in the operating room may display new information. The student may receive feedback in the form of images and sounds, or be prompted for a decision through a dialog box. For example, when the student clicks on the pulse oximeter, the oximeter moves and attaches itself to the patient's finger, and the monitor starts displaying the patient's heartbeat. This approach allows the student to identify when the oximeter should be attached and evaluate its output without having to learn how you would actually move something in Second Life.

As the student works through the induction procedure, making decisions and clicking on equipment, the main controller is recording which equipment the student has activated and which decisions the student has made, as well as the time of these events. The induction procedure is rather complex, and a nurse anesthetist has certain discretion within it. Therefore, the team decided to have faculty evaluate student performance, rather than programming this evaluation and completing it automatically within Second Life. At the end of the simulation, the main controller e-mails all the information to the instructor, who evaluates the student's performance and provides feedback.

Simulation Development Process

KUMC selected Second Life for nurse training because TLT already had experience with this virtual world platform and knew it could provide low-cost, rapid development. The TLT team included two staffers who had experience creating objects in Second Life. One of them also had experience using the Linden Script programming language needed to make these objects interactive. Since the developers did not have an opportunity to work exclusively on the nurse training in Second Life (it was accomplished among their day-to-day activities), it is somewhat difficult to determine precise development time. Approximately one week was devoted to identifying, developing, and refining the four basic object scripts. With initial script development completed, it took about one to two hours to develop a new equipment object and slightly modify the script needed for that object.

Not surprisingly, the most difficult part of development was coordinating schedules with very busy faculty members. To create and tune up the simulation, the TLT team had to learn the induction process themselves, build and script equipment objects, and then meet with NURA faculty to evaluate the new simulation components. This was an iterative process requiring frequent meetings and revisions from both departments. Faculty carefully examined procedures to determine if each of them was realistic enough for the student to learn all the steps properly. Another difficult part of the project was the number and placement of prompts. The prompts are necessary to help learners make sure they know what they have done, where they are at in the procedure, and what they need to do next.

The virtual operating room is located on the university's private island in Second Life, KUMC Isle. By purchasing a private island, the university has been able to completely control access to the island, managing security and privacy. All faculty, staff, and student avatars are uniquely linked to their real-life counterparts, and only authorized people can access KUMC Isle. Building, creating objects, and scripting on KUMC Isle is also restricted to designated users.

Prior to college-wide deployment, the operating room simulation was pilot tested with a small group of NURA students who had already completed the course in the physical world. They were in the unique position to compare both traditional and virtual world approaches. The development team sought their input on usability, authenticity, and educational value. The feedback was unanimous: all students considered the simulation very realistic and believed it would really help future generations of students to learn the induction procedure. The pilot project also helped in identifying several usability issues that were promptly corrected.

Students had little difficulty working within Second Life, even though they received only about ten minutes of basic Second Life instruction. Of course, TLT limited training to the essential virtual world features needed in the simulation: moving, focusing, and interacting with objects. Less relevant items, such as creating and customizing an avatar, were avoided. Developers pre-created avatars and opened accounts to save instruction time. This approach eliminated the need for advanced Second Life skills and, in fact, allowed the students, for the most part, to ignore the underlying technology—the ultimate goal of a successful simulation.

From the educational technology perspective, this project has been a success on all counts. NURA has a working simulation that really helps students to learn complex subject matter. The TLT department gained valuable experience designing and developing training simulations in Second Life, along the way pioneering a new technique for learning complex physical procedures in a virtual world. The simulation approach developed by TLT can be used in other fields where trainees need to learn how to use equipment—for example, assembly of an intricate machine, calibration of instruments, troubleshooting, or responding to emergency situations.

Within the coming academic year, Second Life nursing training will be integrated into the NURA first-year curriculum. In the next three years, KUMC and TLT plan to add increased complexity to the simulation—adding additional branching based on patient conditions, as well as developing other simulations for emergency situations that nurse anesthetists will encounter in a real-life operating room.

 ## Conclusions and Best Practices

The next time you interact with a nurse, a salesperson, or a factory floor manager or talk to an engineer, you may be dealing with a person educated in part by working with simulations in a virtual world. At least to some extent, we owe this to the pioneering work of KUMC employees, who established that:

► Second Life provides a working platform for creating complex procedural training simulations. Simulations can consist of dozens of major steps with numerous decision points that, in turn, can branch into additional sub-procedures based on the learner's actions. Such simulations help students to learn complex procedural steps in a safe and controlled learning space.

► In spite of the absence of the physical "how-to" aspects and physical feedback, the immersive setting provides ample opportunities to learn the sequence of the steps and the branching of decision making. Separating these parameters reduces the cognitive load for the students and improves the overall result by breaking a complex procedure into manageable units.

► A three-dimensional physical environment can be modeled accurately and realistically in Second Life. As a result, trainees can subconsciously learn important parameters of a procedure, such as the location of equipment and materials in a real environment.

▶ Second Life provides programming tools allowing users to record the learner's name, actions, and equipment used, as well as the time of the actions. The instructor can access this information to evaluate the student's performance and provide feedback. In simple simulations, evaluation can be done automatically or semiautomatically. In more complex simulations, human interpretation of the results may be required.

▶ As often happens with technology, the most difficult part of developing a complex simulation is the interaction and coordination among *human* participants at all levels. Programmers and developers have to learn the procedure they are modeling and build and script equipment objects, while subject knowledge experts must evaluate simulation components. This is an iterative process requiring great communication on all sides, in addition to a well-defined common vision.

▶ Prior to enterprise-wide deployment of a simulation, test it with a small group of employees, particularly those who may be able to compare the old training process with the new approach. Identify and correct problems.

▶ The learning curve for using Second Life appears to be less of an issue, especially with younger employees, than it is often made out to be. Limit training to essential virtual world features needed in the simulation: moving, focusing, and interacting with objects. Avoid less relevant items, such as creating and customizing an avatar. Whenever possible, pre-create avatars for learners so that they do not spend instruction time opening accounts or customizing avatars. This approach eliminates the necessity to learn advanced Second Life skills, allowing learners to concentrate on the subject at hand and, for the most part, to ignore the underlying technology.

Recruiting and New-Hire Orientation: TMP Worldwide, EMC Corporation, and IBM Case Studies

What a difference a few months can make! Until the summer of 2008 you could hardly visit a HR-related conference or open a training magazine without hearing or reading about sweeping generational differences, the coming severe shortage of workforce, and how you need to change your recruiting and management to accommodate both and

> " HR should have a seat at the table only if they are able to talk dollars and cents."
> —*Marco Boschetti, consultant, Towers Perrin*

survive. Indeed, with baby boomers expected to start retiring in droves any time, the question of motivating the "What's in it for me?" generation that requires at least two weeks' notice for a one-day business trip reached peak relevance.

Today you are more likely to hear about baby boomers planning to stay at work because their retirement savings disappeared in the market collapse, and millennials complaining about a workplace "logjam" of previous generations. We do not have a magic mirror to tell you where the market will be when you read this book and how it will affect generational differences at the workplace. However, if you reevaluate all that was written and said about boomers, Generation X, and Generation Y, you will probably find that a foundation built on solid HR practices will go a long way in ensuring a rewarding and motivating workplace for all generations of employees.

Nobody but professional market traders on the "bear" side likes a recession. A slow economy levies its toll on everyone, as employers first freeze hiring and then go through massive layoffs. Human resource specialists, who only yesterday were feverishly running after top talent, ready to negotiate for top dollar and perks, all of a sudden find themselves having to negotiate severance packages instead.

Steve Pogorzelski and Jesse Harriott (2007) describe the "Engagement Cycle," which recognizes:

> An employer must continually attract, acquire, and advance talent just as brands attract, acquire, and gain loyalty with customers over time. The Engagement Cycle creates strong bonds between employers and potential candidates before, during, and after the brief period we call "recruiting." Its practices ensure that when the economy strengthens— and talent once again becomes scarce—an employer has built a strong "bench" of talented individuals who are interested, open to discussion, and even grateful for the attention.

The authors go on to describe three phases of the Engagement Cycle:

1. The *attract* phase starts when a candidate first hears or reads about the company and starts to form an impression. This phase can continue for years with various "touch points," such as an advertisement, a story told by a colleague, and so on. It can last for years and may or may not end up growing into the second phase.

2. In the *acquire* phase, the candidate connects to a company in a targeted way using a job advertisement, a network contact, or a call from a recruiter; applies for the job; and goes through the process of getting the job.

3. If the candidate becomes an employee, the *advance* phase starts with all its daily challenges and rewards. It continues until the employee leaves the company for one reason or another.

For our purposes, it is important to recognize that the Engagement Cycle requires a continually executed plan of action targeted at attracting top talent, creating strong relationships with them, and advancing them. In an economic slowdown, both sides of the employment equation—candidates/employees and employers—become significantly more risk-averse than is typical during economic expansion. However, from an organizational perspective, discontinuing the building of long-term relationships with candidates and potential candidates might not be a good idea. It is in difficult times that you need the best specialists the most. Not paying attention to this will definitely come back to haunt organizations when the time to hire returns. In fact, a slowdown offers a rare opportunity to improve corporate branding in the employment marketplace. "Inexpensive actions taken today will make a firm more attractive in the long run to top candidates and boost retention of the best employees" (Pogorzelski and Harriott 2007).

 ## Case Study: TMP Worldwide Uses Second Life to Expand Its Clients' Recruiting Efforts and Branding

An interesting example of using Second Life as one of the tools in the HR arsenal to help support a continuous program of corporate branding was developed by TMP Worldwide—a well-known and well-regarded full-service recruitment advertising agency. As Russell Miyaki, vice president and national interactive creative director, noted, "When revenues slip, payroll comes under severe pressure." Contrary to conventional wisdom, this often only intensifies the war for the top talent—those who can deliver more for each payroll dollar spent. In a recession, smart companies have to present themselves in an attractive light and answer more demanding questions to snag the best candidates. Anything that helps you to break out of the clutter and stand out by communicating your brand as an employer of choice will help. However, spending on the recruiting effort, onboarding, and training is a whole different matter.

You know that a technology has become common when human resources specialists suggest that you use it to attract new talent. TMP Worldwide was the first to take its clients' recruitment efforts into Second Life, using an event called Network in World (NIW). Since this was a global effort involving multinational corporations such as Microsoft, HP, Accenture, EMC, Verizon, Sodexho, IBM, eBay, T-Mobile, US Cellular, and GE, TMP supported the effort from its offices in both the United States and France.

Within its Second Life space, TMP designed and developed a virtual building for each company, to be used for real-time virtual interviews with the candidates. The differences in companies and their corporate cultures was reflected in the buildings: some companies wanted a slick brick-and-mortar representation, while others wanted the building and the experience to represent the "spirit" of their brand and be less literal. In-house personnel and an outside contractor completed building for all the participants within a month and a half. In building virtual world environments, TMP's approach mirrored its procedures for Web and digital development—from discovery to generating strategic scope to creating blueprints to forming creative concepts and producing designs.

The virtual career fair lasted for three days. Event hours were scheduled to accommodate people from different time zones. Each company staffed its building with up to six recruiters whose role was to greet, meet, and interview candidates. There were private interview rooms in every building where a candidate and a recruiter could meet without distractions. The candidates had the option to use text or voice. To keep chats private, they would simply use the "instant message" mode built into Second Life.

Obviously, none of those preparations would make any sense if high-quality candidates did not know about or did not attend the fair. To help ensure the high quality of applicants, TMP developed a website to register, promote, and prescreen candidates before the virtual career fair started.

The site provided vital information about each company, the event, and directions to get to the fair location in Second Life. Candidates were asked to submit their resumes so companies could work in their normal pattern, prescreening the candidates before inviting them to the virtual career fair. Once the candidate was screened and approved, he or she received an invitation with a link and scheduled time. Candidates who did not have a Second Life account were directed to sign up and create an avatar.

Training was a critical component that TMP offered to company recruiters as well as to candidates who had never used Second Life before. It took place through scheduled sessions held weeks in advance of the event itself. Company recruiters were taught using private lessons in Second Life ("in-world" in Second Life lingo). These lessons included everything recruiters needed, from basics (moving around, exchanging instant messages, using voice chat) to advanced topics, such as virtual interview etiquette.

On the day of the event, candidates arrived via the link to the NIW island at a central courtyard staging area where they were greeted by one of the TMP facilitators and guided to their respective appointments. To make navigation as effortless as possible, TMP positioned teleport signs in the courtyard to assist candidates with getting to their appointments. Candidates would simply click on the corresponding signs to get to the correct location. Since the event was spread across two Second Life islands and many of the candidates had limited experience in Second Life, the teleport signs proved to be a simple but very important solution to many novices' problems.

A virtual ground crew of six to eight TMP staffers was positioned throughout the islands to help candidates with everything from navigating and answering quick questions to making sure that they got to their appointment. Just as they would during a real-world job fair event, the TMP team maintained communication with each other (in the NIW events via conference call) as they helped candidates and clients throughout the event.

Once the candidate made it to his or her appointment, the candidate was greeted by a recruiter and then directed to one of the meeting rooms inside the client's building. Often the candidate had time to explore all the branded features inside each building to obtain more information. Some of those branded features were streaming videos about the company and clickable posters that provided detailed information on benefits, culture, and locations; diversity data; job listings; slide shows; and career site links. There were also branded features unique to each company and its Second Life experience. For example, Verizon used the opportunity to leverage its FiOS broadband service brand. TMP created a virtual fiber-optic roller coaster just outside of its building. Candidates were able to take their avatar for a wild ride hanging from a glowing orb that was attached to the fiber-optic rail. As they rode the coaster, they flew by career-branded billboards.

T-mobile wanted to emphasize its message of a risk-taking, fun, adventurous culture by offering candidates virtual skydiving. Candidates were given T-mobile branded virtual parachutes and could launch high into the sky from the top of the T-Mobile building.

The virtual job fair could not fully replace the traditional interview process. It served as an invitation to establish the relationships with potential candidates located throughout North America and around the world. If, during the interview in Second Life, a recruiter felt a specific candidate was worth pursuing to the next step, the recruiter would schedule a real-world meeting.

TMP didn't exclusively target Second Life regulars or outsiders. The audience included both. The age range for most candidates fell between twenty-six and thirty-two. NIW candidates represented all types of skill sets: IT, engineers, telesales, marketers, artists, Web designers, and even chefs. Even though this was an invitation-only event, TMP wanted to avoid the perception of being a big agency imposing its rules and so left the island open to the public and welcomed anyone in the Second Life community who was interested in the event. If a candidate showed up without an appointment, he or she was advised on the best way to get an interview.

As with any real-world event, there were procedures for crisis management. If visitors displayed any inappropriate behavior, such as bad language, harassment, and so on, a TMP staffer was notified and the offender was asked to leave. If the person persisted, he or she was ejected and banned from the island. Otherwise, candidates and visitors were expected to follow general business etiquette rules. This was part of the reason why the event was so rich, fun, and for the most part relaxing. There were very few incidents, none of them serious.

There were many factors of success. The hires were made, the unique databases of candidates were filled, and enormous PR and awareness had been delivered. When you look at the numbers, three days of the virtual job fair offered impressive returns (see Table 11.1).

The virtual world job fair was not meant to replace traditional interviewing, but TMP's experience supports the benefits of its use. This type of recruiting:

- ▶ offers more efficient reach of candidates across geographies
- ▶ allows for deeper branding experiences to the candidates than a traditional job fair booth
- ▶ provides a better platform to connect and screen for both candidates and employers to initiate further interviews. This, in turn, creates a deeper understanding and relationships between a recruiter and a candidate, enabling more quality hires.

TABLE 11.1

	Event 1: eBay, T-Mobile, Microsoft, Sodexho, Verizon, HP	*Event 2: EMC, US Cellular, Accenture, GE Money*
Unique visitors to the NiW site	37,202	24,384
Unique job seekers registered	872	1,004
Job seekers who requested interviews	749	411
Job seekers who were accepted for an interview by the employer	209	101
Job seekers interviewed	144	74

The average investment for a company to participate in the virtual career fair was between $10,000 and $25,000—a significant cost avoidance compared to a traditional job fair in the physical world, which involves time-consuming and expensive travel, transportation of the booths across the country, and other costs. And often the quality of candidates is significantly worse than those who showed up for the virtual world job fair.

Finally, there was an unexpected but welcome side effect: the project enhanced collaboration and training within TMP as well as within clients' organizations.

Case Study: EMC Corporation Uses Second Life to Boost Company Brand as an Employer of Choice

EMC Corporation is a technology company whose name—like Cisco, Microsoft, Intel, IBM, or Oracle—constitutes a well-known brand. To a large degree, its continued success depends on the company's ability to attract talented, highly motivated employees.

According to Polly Pearson, vice president of employment brand and strategy engagement, in recent years EMC has been hiring between nine thousand and ten thousand people per year. For those of us who have ever faced the problem of finding and hiring one or two gifted people, the task of finding and enticing several thousand exceptional employees might seem overwhelming. Competitive salaries, bonus programs, excellent benefits, and growth and development opportunities are all necessary ingredients in creating the compelling and rewarding work environment that the real talent is looking for. However, unless you succeed in branding your company as *the* place to work, the real talent will select other opportunities. Moreover, if you think that the task becomes easier during an economic downturn, think again.

Second Life immediately appealed to Pearson as a way to stand out and attract coveted talent, especially "passive" talent. These are people who are generally accomplished, are successful at what they do, and are not actively seeking new employment. Along with other advantages, EMC saw Second Life as a tool that would help the company to reinforce its brand as an innovative, vibrant, and creative technology company, appealing to the best of the best. An attractive price point helped as well, so when EMC was approached by TMP Worldwide, it seized the opportunity even though at the time there was no budget.

In the physical world, career fairs seem to be a common and well-rehearsed way to reach the widest pool of talent in a meaningful way. You select a promising city, rent a place, advertise, advertise, advertise, advertise more, buy muffins and coffee, pray there is no snowstorm or flood, collect resumes, and interview people who showed up from the vicinity of that city.

In Second Life the process is somewhat simpler. You create and equip a meeting place (you can do it once for all your needs), advertise, schedule interviews, and then greet people from around the world—almost immediately. Although EMC promoted its career fairs only in the United States, qualified candidates from Japan, the Netherlands, and Great Britain showed up. One of the most remarkable candidates was from Arkansas—not a place where EMC would regularly hold a career fair or look for an expert. She was an accomplished Silicon Valley tech writer who had left Silicon Valley for family reasons. If not for Second Life, it is highly unlikely she would ever have had the opportunity to attend an EMC career fair.

For the first career fair, EMC partnered with TMP Worldwide. Using EMC's specifications, TMP created a virtual EMC HQ as a round, translucent structure with vibrant colors, located on the TMP Second Life island. Again, in a virtual world a building does not have to be brick and square; rather, it can reflect the essence of your brand.

Advertising through regular channels brought approximately 150 resumes; about 50 out of them were selected for an interview. Of those interviewed, 40 percent were asked for second-round interviews—indicating an unusually high proportion of qualified candidates. Ultimately, there was so much buzz that many qualified people just showed up without an appointment and were eventually interviewed. While waiting, people could view a movie about EMC's business and what it is like to work for EMC, and many examined the company's value propositions and opportunities.

The main result of the first career fair EMC held in Second Life was a successful "proof of concept." The company confirmed that Second Life is a viable platform for recruiting. This initial success prompted EMC to run a second career fair two months later. This time it felt comfortable enough with the technology to run the event on its own, especially since the building was fully established and recruiters were trained and already familiar with running this type of event. Prior to the second career fair EMC received more than three hundred resumes. Of those interviewed, 80 percent were called for a second interview. EMC ultimately made two hires from this event. One hire was an engineer with highly coveted operating system expertise; the other was a financial controller with a background on a global, Fortune 500 scale.

When EMC launched its activities with Second Life as an employment branding vehicle, it expected to further EMC's brand image as an innovative and dynamic high-tech company, increase the attraction of elusive talent to EMC as a place to work, and fill job openings with the type of talent who would thrive at EMC.

The Second Life career fairs met these objectives and accomplished more than that. Positive discoveries about Second Life for EMC included:

▶ **Relationship acceleration and community building.** Second Life adds energy, interest, and excitement to every interaction. It makes use of sight, sound, and tactile senses and manages to fully immerse people into an immediately engaging, interactive environment. As such, it is much more "rich and fascinating" than a phone call, an e-mail, a webcam, or even an in-person meeting. The interaction between interviewer and candidate in a virtual world creates a feeling of familiarity that often requires several meetings to achieve in the physical world. At the end of the career fair, after a group photo, none of the EMC staff wanted to leave, and it was 11:00 P.M. on a work night!

▶ **Inclusion and equal footing.** People arrived in the color, shape, age, sexual orientation, and gender in which they wished to be seen. For recruiters, it allowed frank discussions of both the prospect's qualifications and the company's opportunities, helping to match both sides of the equation.

▶ **Multiple talent dimensions.** People from multiple disciplines such as sales, marketing, finance, human resources, and professional services— *in addition* to engineering—applied to be interviewed in this forum.

▶ **Another promotional dimension to a resume.** The candidates' avatars allowed a level of self-expression not often found in real-world interviews. Candidates applying for sales positions tended to arrive in suits, with briefcases. People applying for engineering positions often arrived in T-shirts, shorts, and a goatee; one person arrived dressed as Superman. A public relations candidate arrived in a flowing summer dress with a coordinating wide-brimmed hat.

▶ **Personal brand elevation.** Candidates who were interviewed "in-world" had the ultimate conversation starter for months to come, further spreading the word about EMC.

▶ **Significant cost avoidance.** EMC avoided costs in the form of saved time, increased flexibility, and agility. Thanks to a onetime investment in building Second Life infrastructure, EMC can now hold career fairs with three days' notice without incurring extra costs.

It is interesting to note that although some candidates already were Second Life residents, a significant number of qualified people were new to Second Life and had to open an account in order to take part in the career fair. From the company's perspective, this has been a very positive finding.

EMC is not only a technology leader but a learning company as well. Eighty percent of its revenue in any given year comes from products that it invented in the prior eighteen months. Prospective employees *must* be intellectually excited by the prospect of continuous learning if they want to survive and thrive at EMC. In truth, the ability to constantly reinvent your skill set and never lose your curiosity and desire to learn is expected in every job. Candidates lacking these capabilities will not do well in the company, even if they have a respectable resume. In this regard, Second Life helped EMC reach coveted passive talent that fits its culture.

Case Study: IBM China Successfully Moves New-Hire Orientation to Virtual Worlds

There are plenty of reasons why IBM is known as a technology leader. We will venture to say that one of these reasons is that the company is quick to recognize promising new developments and start experimenting with new technologies, while others remain "on the fence" waiting for tangible results from the "first adopters." Today Big Blue works on at least fourteen active projects in different areas of virtual world use, in various geographic locations, using several different virtual world platforms. At least three of these projects are testing the applicability of virtual world platforms in the human resources management area.

Recruiting and new-hire orientation present special challenges when there is a very large number of applicants. This often happens in China, where IBM launched "Blue Pathway"—a special program for large-scale internship training and new-hire orientation. Each year IBM China receives thousands of job applications from the top university graduates. Nearly all of them are highly qualified and motivated young people, so selecting the best of the best is no small task. Similarly, simultaneous orientation and onboarding of a large number of highly qualified but inexperienced new employees is another quite difficult and resource-consuming mission.

In 2008 IBM China experimented with two virtual world platforms (Second Life and Active Worlds) in an attempt to make new-hire orientation more efficient. The program aimed to provide an immersive experience in IBM culture, history, and organization and promote team spirit by collaboration in the virtual world. Almost six hundred recent college graduates took part in the program. The company also used virtual worlds for training, including customer training and "soft" marketing—educating the public about the company.

The project was developed by the IBM China Human Resources team, the IBM Center for Advanced Learning, and the IBM China Research Lab. After the project was approved and funded, the company developed the virtual world environments using internal IBM resources over the course of three months. To orient the participants in the virtual worlds, the company conducted extensive training. It designed two major learning activities:

1. Blue Pathway Exhibition Hall. The exhibition hall was a three-dimensional space allowing candidates to review IBM history, organization, values, career development, securities, and other relevant information.

2. Blue Pathway Summer Island. The island was a team-based content co-creation project. The virtual world project group was split into several teams that planned, designed, and developed contents on separate parts of the island. Competing teams presented their results during the final review meeting.

As often happens with established, mature organizations, IBM executives were somewhat concerned that using a virtual world as a platform for a serious project would be seen more as a game and less as a training and orientation event. These doubts proved to be unjustified, for the participants appreciated the opportunity to use new tools, and productivity was higher than when using other methods of instruction. New hires could see IBM offices in different countries around the globe, meet their peers and colleagues from all over the world, and learn more efficiently about IBM products and services.

Along with synchronous methods, such as meetings, IBM used asynchronous e-learning tools and materials that new employees could access for self-study at any time. The company also organized team-building, collaboration, and leadership-building activities that strengthened corresponding skills and helped new employees build horizontal and vertical relationships faster than would other methods.

Post-project interviews revealed a high level of satisfaction with the program among the participants as a "smart, efficient, and interesting way" to orient new hires within the big global company, without having to move them all to a single physical location. At the same time, the company reports "tremendous cost savings compared to conducting an event in the real world" and "significant measurable reduction in spending required to orient new hires." As a result, IBM plans to continue the program, perhaps testing other virtual worlds and leveraging the two learning activities it had used. The stated objective is to continue to expand and enhance the program over the coming years.

 ## Conclusions and Best Practices

Human resources rarely receives accolades when business runs smoothly. But when there is a serious problem, it can often be traced back to HR errors, reminding everyone how expensive these errors can be. Obviously, virtual worlds are not a panacea for all HR problems, but using them helps make hiring and recruiting more effective, while at the same time allowing you to cast your net wider and find better-qualified people.

► Second Life has become widespread enough to make it a cost-effective tool for recruiting and new-hire orientation. In a virtual world, organizations can find specialists in multiple, not necessarily technical, disciplines such as sales, marketing, finance, human resources, and professional services—in addition to engineering.

► Second Life provides an opportunity for a company to break out of the clutter and stand out from its competitors, communicating its brand as an employer in an attractive light.

► Companies can project their corporate culture in the content that they create in a virtual world, which in turn helps them to attract the right candidates for the job.

► Virtual worlds add energy, interest, and excitement to every interaction. The interaction between an interviewer and a candidate in a virtual world creates a feeling of familiarity and trust. People choose the color, shape, age, sexual orientation, and gender in which they wish to be seen. In terms of recruiting, it leads to frank discussions of both the prospect's qualifications and the company's opportunities, helping to match both sides of the equation.

► Using virtual worlds as a platform for recruiting and new-hire orientation can help companies realize significant cost avoidance. A one-time investment in building virtual world infrastructure is all that's required for an organization to use it for any number of future events, including career fairs, orientation sessions, team- and leadership-building activities, intracompany collaboration, and more, at no extra cost.

► Even if a candidate does not have a Second Life account or experience in a virtual world, an invitation to try it might work exceptionally well for a leader company that seeks individuals willing and able to learn new things. If your company requires prospective employees to be intellectually excited by learning and developing new skills, virtual world recruiting might be a great fit for you.

▶ Use a Web interface and Second Life tools to schedule interviews in Second Life.

▶ Train the company staffers in everything they might need for running the events in a virtual world: from basics (moving around, exchanging instant messages, using voice chat) to more advanced topics, such as virtual interview etiquette.

▶ Staff your Second Life location with trained people. It is a good idea to publish a schedule of staffers' availability both on the Web and in Second Life.

▶ Use different technologies and modes of communication. Create private areas for interviews so that a candidate and a recruiter feel comfortable discussing confidential matters. Make sure different modes of communication—such as in-world voice, text, and instant messaging—are available. Instruct candidates and staffers to use the instant messaging tool to keep chat private.

▶ Prescreen candidates before a virtual career fair starts, and collect resumes using in-world and Web tools or e-mail.

▶ Provide vital information about the company. Have branded features for candidates to explore, such as streaming videos about the company and clickable posters with detailed information on benefits, culture, and locations; diversity data; job listings; slide shows; and career site links. You do not need to create all of these features from scratch. Current HR and marketing materials can be converted into formats usable in Second Life.

▶ Provide links from the Web directly to your Second Life location. Make navigation as effortless as possible by creating teleport signs.

▶ A Second Life interview is not a replacement of a regular hiring process but rather a way to prescreen candidates and select the right ones for the next step. If you feel the candidate is worth pursuing, set up a real-world meeting.

▶ Set up procedures for crisis management. If anyone displays inappropriate behavior, ask the offender to leave. If the person persists, eject him or her and ban the person from the island.

▶ Do not stop at recruiting. Create a secure access area for new hires to help them with orientation and onboarding. Encourage older colleagues to meet their new peers and offer support and mentoring.

▶ Use both synchronous events and asynchronous e-learning tools and materials that new employees can use for self-study at any time.

Enterprise Collaboration: The Virtual World Application

Solutions for business activities such as sales, marketing, human resources management, information technology, and many others rely on efficient, cost-effective, multidirectional—but not necessarily formal—business collaboration. As Thomas Davenport pointed out in 2005, before Second Life became well known in the corporate world, the most competent 40 percent of knowledge workers learned most of the important information from social networks (Davenport 2005).

> "In the long history of humankind (and animal kind, too) those who learned to collaborate and improvise most effectively have prevailed."
> —*Charles Darwin*

Robert Cohen (2008) recently noted that in the world of business, collaboration has become an important tool in reducing time to market and increasing cost savings. "The rise of the collaborative enterprise that is likely to result from the successful deployment of Virtual World technologies will usher in a new era of business. It will change the way firms compete with one another for customers in both goods and services industries . . . [and] encourage a more collaborative and enterprising form of business" (Cohen 2008). Since Dale Dougherty and Craig Cline coined the term "Web 2.0" in 2004, describing the World Wide Web as a platform for interconnected interactive content, many authors have supported the concept and provided experimental data detailing how Web 2.0 tools help in business collaboration (for example, see the references in Davenport 2005).

When it comes to virtual worlds, until recently authors have limited themselves to saying that "Web 3D immersive environments *are likely* to transform the environment for collaboration by providing for the immediate exchange of ideas and sophisticated analyses" (Cohen 2008; emphasis ours) simply because there was no experimental work available to prove or disprove the point.

Thanks to the work of a group of researchers from Penn State and Indiana University (Social Science Research Institute, Pennsylvania State University 2008; TechRadar 2008) and a team of scientists from North Carolina and Indiana Universities (Massey and Montoya 2008; Massey et al. 2009) this is no longer the case. In both cases researchers studied how different collaboration tools affected the results of competing teams of students. In the first case, teams of students were asked to solve a complex problem, using different meeting scenarios: ten teams worked face-to-face, ten teams worked through teleconferencing, and twelve teams worked as groups of avatars in Second Life. The researchers found that the "face-to-face teams felt most confident of their performance, yet the Second Life teams provided the most accurate answers in the task" (TechRadar 2008).

In the second study (Massey et al. 2009), the teams worked on developing a business case for service innovations for two Fortune 500 companies. The researchers selected a very interesting, more lifelike approach. Just as businesses and employees in real life have a selection of tools to complete a task, students in the experiment were free to select what tools they wished to use. Any of the tools out of these three groups were freely and equally available to all student teams:

▶ **Group 1 tools:** traditional, including face-to-face meetings and Web 1.0 tools such as e-mail and file depositories

➤ **Group 2 tools:** Web 2.0 tools, including wikis and blogs
➤ **Group 3 tools:** a virtual world platform—Second Life

In spite of an opportunity to freely select any advanced tools, there were teams who defaulted to the tools that were most familiar to them, mostly those in Group 1. Others chose a combination of Group 1 and Group 2 tools, and the most "adventurous" (or, more likely, the most advanced) used tools from all three groups. The researchers came to three major conclusions:

1. Greater or exclusive reliance on older technologies such as e-mail and document repositories negatively correlates with team performance. Newer technologies, such as Second Life, are positively correlated with team success, especially when used together with Web 2.0 tools.

2. Second Life played a key role in the development of social relationships among team members, which were critical to team performance. Second Life also proved to be a good platform for holding decision-making discussions.

3. Availability of collaborative technologies does not necessarily lead to their adoption in the workplace. Several teams in the study did not take advantage of the new technology.

Massey and Montoya (2008) obtained feedback from the participants to see how they felt the different tools and technologies helped them achieve their tasks:

Analysis of student feedback from a post-course assessment survey confirms that Second Life played a key role in the collaborative work of the student teams. While each team worked independently and could use whatever technologies it preferred, the feedback indicates that students relied heavily on Second Life for developing and building team relationships—known to be essential to team project success—and for holding decision-making discussions. Other tools, such as wikis and document repositories, complemented the capabilities of Second Life—for example, providing the means to write, edit, share, and store project-related documents. Results also show that the use of Second Life directly influenced project performance and teamwork satisfaction.

While research shows that new tools and technologies can be very useful in the workplace, they do not necessarily get adopted automatically. Organizations must make an effort to educate their employees about the new technologies and promote their use.

Expanding Enterprise Collaboration: Cisco Live in the Second Life TechChat Series

Only an ongoing effort to manage effective learning and development goals can ensure that employee development is always in line with strategic organizational objectives. Effective collaboration connects players and processes across the enterprise. People can quickly test-drive ideas, capture experience and knowledge, form horizontal cross-functional informal and semiformal teams, and meet project deadlines across geographic and departmental boundaries. At the same time, as organizations face the coming demographic shift due to the retirement of "boomers," they need to capture shared knowledge in order to minimize knowledge gaps and preserve intellectual capital.

As a leader in new communications and business tools, Cisco internally discussed the strategy and benefits of moving a number of real-life activities into virtual environments. According to Dannette Veale, new media program manager at Cisco, the company is a strong believer in the future of corporate virtual worlds. As a first step, Cisco decided to take advantage of the Second Life environment as an opportunity to communicate and collaborate with customers and partners. There was also a good technical motivation for the company to try a three-dimensional environment, as engineers saw a major opportunity in adding a third dimension to the current two-dimensional "flat" Internet. From a technical standpoint, they saw virtual worlds as an extremely useful tool in troubleshooting complex network configuration issues.

TechChat became the first "proof of concept" project to use Second Life for communication and collaboration among Cisco employees and their customers and partners. It became the first opportunity to validate the strategic direction that the company has adopted in the area of collaboration.

During different stages of the project, between three and ten employees—representing the marketing, events, communications, business development, training, and recruiting departments—have been part of the Cisco virtual world task force. It is interesting to note that the employees participating in the project have ranged in age from thirty to fifty, but there have been no significant differences in the level of platform adoption among employees belonging to different generations. In the process of selecting a platform, the Cisco task force tried one event in test mode in Google's (now defunct) virtual world platform, Lively, but were not impressed, so they moved to Second Life.

The first mission of the Second Life team was to create a collaborative environment to support Cisco customers. The team created multiple-use venues that utilized text chat, integrated voice, in-world PowerPoint-type presentations, streaming audio for the presentations, and multimedia displays for relevant content. Even internal proponents of Second Life were surprised by how quickly this virtual world became a preferred platform for technical collaboration, support, and meetings, changing corporate focus in corresponding areas.

Success in the corporate use of Second Life prompted the company to create automated training for employees who had no prior experience in Second Life. At the same time, Cisco made it a rule to conduct hands-on training sessions for presenters and staff prior to all events that Cisco holds in Second Life.

As with all companies venturing into Second Life, the Cisco team is under strong pressure to prevent any breaches of company security.

Understandably, this pressure is much stronger in technology companies, where network security is a critical part of business operations. To prevent network intrusions, the team decided to use what is becoming a common security arrangement: within the company you can reach Second Life only via an external proxy or by using a guest network. Within Second Life, Cisco has separate "free access" and "employee-only" environments to manage and maintain access privileges and security.

There is another important security feature utilized by Cisco that, so far, has not received the attention it deserves in other companies. Linden Lab, the creator of Second Life, controls all last names of avatars. Regularly, new users select a last name out of the list of available names; however, it is possible to license a custom last name that will be available only to your organization's employees. Cisco licensed the last name "CiscoSystems" for exclusive use by all its employees.

It is easy to create a Second Life "group" and include only employees from your organization in that group. It is also easy to allow access to certain areas only to members of a certain group. This is called "access-list" security—you create lists of people who can access a certain area. At the same time, when in Second Life, you can see the other avatars' names as a "tag" above their heads. As a result, if all employees have a custom last name, any intruder attempting to access an "employee-only" area will easily be spotted even if he or she was able to overcome access-list security. Computer security experts agree that the best way to protect a site is by using a multilayer approach and verifying privileges by using differentiating credentials. Having avatars from your organization assigned the same last name creates an additional level of protection that is easy to create and hard to breach.

Perhaps due to its attention to detail, Cisco reports no problems with griefers. As for employee conduct, Cisco adheres to its regular employee code of conduct and reports no violations, difficulties, or problems, even though it has held events that attracted very large numbers of people with numerous interactions.

Hundreds (in the case of regular live events) to thousands (special events) of network engineers, software developers, and network business managers have been involved in TechChat on the customer side. All of them were highly technical professionals who took part in the Cisco-organized events to discuss specific questions and to collaborate with their peers and Cisco representatives.

Customers seem to be very pleased with the work they can perform and the technical support they receive in Second Life. The perceived "coolness" of the venue seems to play little role, as customers use the platform to work and not to enjoy playing with the latest gadget. In turn, customer satisfaction led to rapid adoption of the Second Life platform within Cisco. Within some of the departments, the adoption level—the number of Cisco employees involved in the Second Life project—tripled between 2007 and 2008.

Today the company is working to install enhanced registration management capabilities for its centralized virtual environment. It also plans to have more events that build on an ongoing narrative, as opposed to stand-alone one-off events. Cisco is also reviewing a proposal to test employee participation in a more game-oriented space such as World of Warcraft.

 ## Marketing as a Collaborative Activity

When organizations design and execute initiatives out of context, disconnected from the rest of the business, they often lose out on opportunities. If they happen to use a new technology for such a project, it might become the "culprit," as disappointment in the results translates into disappointment in the technology. Only by managing effective learning and development goals in an ongoing effort can companies ensure that employee development is in line with strategic organizational objectives.

Marketing seems to be the one business activity that is often misunderstood in the virtual world environment. Original attempts at marketing in Second Life led to poor results, as well-intentioned but inexperienced virtual world pioneers quickly found out that avatars, while *similar* to people, *are not people*, and although a three-dimensional virtual world has similarities with the already familiar Web, there are significant differences as well. Based on their World Wide Web experience, some corporate early adopters planned their initial Second Life projects to "establish presence" in the virtual world.

While these projects initially received significant publicity, they quickly fizzled, unable to attract and hold on to Second Life residents who had nothing to do in the overpriced copies of real-life hotels and corporate headquarters. Avatars do not need to sleep, unless you log into Second Life and get distracted. (After several minutes of inactivity, your avatar will "fall asleep" so that others see that you are not immediately available.) Certainly, avatars do not need a hotel, a room, and a bed to sleep in. Building a luxury hotel on a nice island in Second Life as a marketing ploy to bring avatars to spend a weeklong vacation on your property will fail. Since the building of such a structure requires a lot of work, it will be an expensive failure, too.

Others tried using Second Life in a way perhaps too close to the physical world—for example, providing reading materials in the form of a book. I remember purchasing one such book about Second Life basics a few days after I signed up for the Second Life account. It was a total disaster. It took me another day just to figure out how to open that book, and when I finally did, reading it was an impossible, eye-wrecking exercise.

When the cavalier attitudes such as "We are great on the Web and the same approach will work fine in Second Life," or "This is so-o-o cool; we will establish presence and our customers will come" failed, the resulting overcorrection almost buried the corporate use of virtual worlds for two to three years. Luckily, there were companies that managed to avoid these pitfalls. Slowly but deliberately they moved ahead, trying new use cases. As a result, today we have a much better understanding of the possibilities made available by the new medium. The uses of Second Life for collaborative work, communication, disseminating information, technical support, and educating customers are very promising new directions.

With a better understanding that collaboration is one of the strongest areas of virtual worlds came the understanding that marketing, in fact, can and will work in Second Life. Second Life marketing is by nature collaborative and is closer to customer education and spreading information in a way that engages a customer, rather than the typical "click-through-and-get-something" Internet marketing. The World Bank took this direction in developing its experimental but highly successful Second Life marketing program.

Case Study: World Bank Uses Second Life to Advance "Doing Business" Report

The World Bank is not a bank in the common sense of the word. It consists of two international organizations jointly owned by 185 member countries—the International Bank for Reconstruction and Development (IBRD) and the International Development Association (IDA). While the former focuses on middle-income and creditworthy poor countries, the latter works with the poorest countries in the world. Together they try to advance the vision of inclusive and sustainable economic development around the world. The organization provides low-interest and interest-free loans for education, health, public administration, infrastructure, financial- and private-sector development, and other vital areas.

Faced with growing demands for greater transparency and accountability in its work, the World Bank finds it extremely important to spread information about its real work, how it operates around the world, and what are the concrete results of the projects completed with the help of its loans and grants. One of the World Bank flagship reports is an annual report called "Doing Business." It ranks 181 economies on the ease of doing business and highlights the importance of regulatory reforms in giving businesses better opportunities to grow and create jobs.

"Doing Business" provides objective measures of business regulations and their enforcement across 181 economies and selected cities. It ranks economies based on ten indicators that record the time and cost necessary to meet government requirements in starting and operating a business, trading across borders, paying taxes, and closing a business. The rankings do not reflect macroeconomic policy, quality of infrastructure, currency volatility, investor perceptions, or crime rates.

With the help of government officials, nongovernmental organizations, lawyers, academics, and the private sector, the findings of the "Doing Business" reports have been extensively disseminated through "road shows" in more than fifty countries. Ramin Aliyev, a business analyst in the World Bank Group's Financial and Private Sector Development Vice Presidency and a major proponent of using Second Life for business, believes that in the twenty-first century, a virtual world is a crucial venue to complement an effective outreach campaign.

In 2008 the World Bank tested Second Life as a platform for disseminating "Doing Business" and the information it contains. The organization wanted to reach new audiences around the world—particularly policymakers, business owners, investors, aid donors, and the general public—through social media. The World Bank believed that the more people could learn about the report and contribute to a global business dialogue aimed at stimulating reforms that improve business environments, the more business start-ups, job opportunities, and economic growth would ultimately be created.

More than eight hundred Second Life residents from around the world participated in the launch of the report. Fifteen to twenty of them introduced themselves as journalists, representatives from academia, and social media experts, while others preferred to remain anonymous and identified themselves as people simply interested in the World Bank and globalization. Visitors had heard about the Doing Business launch in Second Life through World Bank's prelaunch outreach campaign.

Not surprisingly, the World Bank does not have on staff Second Life designers, programmers, or PR specialists familiar with virtual worlds. The company outsourced all Second Life–specific work: marketing, design, staffing, and development for the report launch and two supporting events. Once the management approved the project, the vendor team led by Joni West started working with the World Bank project team to flesh out the project requirements, build a virtual environment, market the events four weeks ahead of the launch, and organize post-launch interviews with prominent websites such as Metanomics and RealBiz in Second Life that prepare and broadcast virtual world shows over the Web. It took about two weeks to build the Doing Business venue in Second Life, and another three weeks to market and organize the event logistics.

Initial funding for the project was at the "experimental" level (more precise information cannot be provided here due to a nondisclosure agreement between the World Bank and the vendor). Although the Doing Business team was present in Second Life for a few days in October 2008, the vendor agreed to keep the venue up through December 2008 at no additional cost. This gave interested parties a great opportunity to visit the World Bank Group team in Second Life for interviews and discussions.

On October 30, 2008, Dahlia Khalifa, a senior strategy adviser of the World Bank Group's Doing Business project, hosted a one-hour Second Life live event presenting the findings of the "Doing Business" report and answering questions. Khalifa's avatar was standing on the stage and going through the presentation slides, a similar format to real-life events the World Bank had previously conducted to promote its report. All the participants sat in a theater-style arrangement and could clearly see Khalifa's slides and listen to her presentation through a live audio stream.

Another member of the World Bank Group team, Ryan Hahn, a consultant for the World Bank Group's Financial and Private Sector Development Vice Presidency, collected questions from the participants through instant messaging. The team received fifteen questions pertaining to the World Bank in general, the "Doing Business" report, and its Second Life project. At the end of the presentation, Khalifa had a chance to respond to all the questions, and then Khalifa and Hahn invited guests to the next-door virtual café, where they continued conversation in a less formal setting.

Keren Flavell, executive producer of SLCN.TV (www.slcn.tv), "a virtual world television network that broadcasts live shows entirely created inside of 3-D spaces," moderated the presentation. Another company, This Second Marketing LLC, provided virtual security staffing for the event.

To increase interest in the presentation and the new venue, the World Bank used a strategy of growing expectations. Two days prior to the main event, Khalifa and Rebecca Ong, who manages global communications for the World Bank Group's Doing Business project and Financial and Private Sector Development Vice Presidency, hosted a press day for journalists that attracted ten media representatives. The venue also featured an interactive Google map "mashup" called Business Planet (www.business-planet.org). A comprehensive dataset on the ease of doing business in 181 countries was just one click away for the Second Life guests.

One day before the main event, the World Bank hosted a live musical performance at the same venue. Second Life residents were treated to some of Second Life's top entertainments and were able to pick up digital copies of the report's overview, as well as World Bank's virtual apparel and products through kiosks at the event site. The team also ran a quiz, and the first fifty people who correctly answered three questions received five hundred Linden Dollars. Even though this sum is approximately equivalent to two U.S. dollars, this "game money" gave Second Life residents an opportunity to purchase virtual clothes or gadgets and thus provided an inexpensive but nevertheless valuable prize.

Reporters and other interested parties seemed to like the new Second Life venue for the "Doing Business" report presentation. "The World Bank Space provides a small, cozy space for members of the World Bank team to speak with members of the press or other interested parties in a one-on-one setting. It also provides a larger press suite which will be used for press conferences and a world café where people can gather to discuss the 'Doing Business' report and how they might start businesses in new countries" (Huffhines 2008).

As with any global event, finding a time slot acceptable to people from all continents and nearly every time zone was perhaps the hardest part of this project. In addition, the World Bank team found out that its computers had outdated graphics cards and so had to upgrade computers for the Doing Business team members.

In retrospect, the team found out that its plan did not include enough incentives for participants and guests to disclose more of their personal and business information. This could have helped the organization to establish long-lasting relationships with the audience and to improve the return on investment of the project by allowing World Bank to refine its strategies and better target further marketing efforts in the future.

However, there were more positive results. As part of the new approach to outreach, Second Life provided an unparalleled opportunity, attracting more than eight hundred interested visitors to review the new "Doing Business" report. Taking advantage of the ability to easily record Second Life events, the World Bank team recorded several interviews that were posted on YouTube and the Metanomics website. There, these materials have been reviewed by many people who did not have an opportunity to attend the live event. For example, Khalifa's interview posted on YouTube generated more than a thousand views in the first month. The *Chicago Sun Times* and the Second Life News Network ran featured stories about the presentation.

The World Bank team likes to call the attention its project received "a derivative product." Unlike other kinds of financial derivatives, which have received justifiably negative publicity lately, these derivative products of the virtual launch worked quite well and allowed the World Bank to reach a global audience in a more engaging and exciting way. In the longer term, the World Bank is considering replicating some of its real-world forums in Second Life, or perhaps even hosting mixed reality events that will take place as a real-world forum and a Second Life event at the same time.

Conclusions and Best Practices

Sometimes we can get overwhelmed by new technologies and feel a strong urge to stick to the tried and trusted way of doing things. While understandable on a human level, this strategy does not pay in the long run.

► Experimental results received by researchers from North Carolina, Indiana, and Pennsylvania State universities demonstrate that teams relying on a combination of Web 1.0, Web 2.0, and virtual worlds technologies gain significant competitive advantage and achieve greater success than those that use only Web 1.0 or a combination of Web 1.0 and Web 2.0 technologies. Differences in performance are statistically significant and cannot be explained by other factors. Older tools, such as e-mail and document repositories, remain relevant for their narrow areas of use. Outside these narrow areas, appropriate use of the new technologies significantly increases a team's chances of success by increasing the efficiency and quality of work.

► When given equal access to a variety of tools, successful teams see an opportunity to use new technologies (Web 2.0, Second Life) to their advantage, while underperformers stick to "what they know best."

► Second Life was shown to be a crucial element in the sequence from social relationships to team relationships to team performance. It is also shown to be a good platform for holding decision-making discussions. Use other tools that provide the means to write, edit, share, and store project-related documents to complement Second Life.

► Teams preferring and relying exclusively on face-to-face meetings might subjectively feel most confident in their performance. However, objective measurements disprove the validity of that feeling. In fact, these teams failed to match the performance of teams that took advantage of Second Life.

► When working on an enterprise collaboration project, the following rules proved to be useful:
  –Streamline registration and initial experiences.
  –Use custom last names for the avatars of company employees to establish an additional layer of security.

– Do not spend resources building an expensive corporate campus. There is zero value in a virtual copy of your office building.
– Second Life is not the Web. Avoid using it as you would use the Web. Do not use it just with an intent to "create presence." Do not provide hard-to-read text or billboards with so much written information that one could hardly read it. Instead, use interactive tools and events to convey your message.
– Following an event, create several stations where participants can talk to company representatives, ask questions, or discuss subjects of interest.
– When holding marketing events, use a system of growing expectations leading to the day of the event. Start building expectations with a prelaunch outreach campaign.
– Use Second Life and third-party tools to create and broadcast video and audio (see Chapter 5 for the list of available tools). Use broadcasting to the Web to increase the audience. Involve people who cannot yet reach Second Life, and use recordings posted on your corporate site and YouTube to increase the post-event audience.
– Involve both in-world and real-world press and media representatives to spread the word.

The Future of Employee Training in Virtual Worlds

physicist Seth Lloyd recently wrote (Lloyd 2006), "The only way to discover the future is to wait and see what happens." Abraham Lincoln, on the other hand, said, "The best way to predict your future is to create it!" In looking at the future of employee training in virtual worlds, we take the second approach. That is, we look at what is being created in virtual world technology *now* and where it might lead in ten or twenty years.

"My interest is in the future because I am going to spend the rest of my life there."
—Charles F. Kettering, American engineer and inventor of the electric starter, 1876–1958

In the evolution of technological innovations, the actual creation of the technologies comes first, followed by the development of new applications and processes to utilize the new technology. As we all know, the use of a new technology can have profound implications for changing human behaviors both for individuals and for groups. It is in exploiting these changes that new business opportunities arise. Of course, this also has implications for how employees learn about the running of a business, whether by formal training or through interaction with the new devices and applications (and with each other). In this chapter, we summarize the current use of virtual worlds and look at the technical changes we can expect in virtual worlds in the near future. These changes might take place both in individual and group behavior of employees, but they will affect the business as a whole, including the future of employee training.

 # Trends in the Corporate Use of Virtual Worlds

The use of virtual worlds in enterprises is in its early stages. However, we can see some definite trends in how large organizations will use virtual worlds in the near future. These trends include an increase in collaboration among members of virtual teams, specific training programs set up in virtual worlds, and leadership and team development.

Virtual Collaboration

There are many ways to describe the history of humankind in general and the history of industrialization and business in particular. We'd suggest that to a large degree this is the history of two opposite elements: collaboration and competition. From the early stages of commerce, collaboration among employees, suppliers, and customers was a decisive factor in a competitive world. Later, when geographically dispersed workforces became common, the need to retain a competitive edge led first to increased travel and then to stimulated development of remote collaboration tools—from e-mail to remote virtual meetings and desktop sharing applications. Better collaboration translates into more productive work and, according to Booz Allen Hamilton (2006) and Robert Cohen (2008), increases general competitiveness and decreases time to market.

While modern biology does not support Meckel-Serres Law in its general form ("ontogeny recapitulates phylogeny," meaning that advanced species in their development pass through stages represented by adult organisms of more primitive species), it is hard not to see a similar law influencing our relationship with new knowledge. The first thing humans do with a new technology is try to use it in place of and in exactly the same manner as they used the preceding one. As Marshall McLuhan noted (McLuhan and Fiore 1967), our first response to new technologies is to try to make them fit existing processes. "We look at the present through a rear-view mirror. We march backwards into the future," said McLuhan.

Just as attempts to use the World Wide Web for business often started with placing scanned versions of a sales brochure on a company website, the first attempts of using virtual worlds for business consisted of building a copy of a corporate campus, a bank, or a hotel in Second Life in hopes that that these reproductions of real life would attract potential customers. Just as in the real world, where business collaboration started with meetings and presentations, the first examples of business collaboration we saw in virtual worlds were meetings and presentations using slide-show screens. While it is obvious by now that simply building a copy of your office in Second Life is about as useful as putting a scanned version of a sales brochure on your website in hopes of attracting new business, meetings and presentations *do* have a valid place in virtual worlds.

Stopping there, however, would be similar to stopping at the "scanned brochure" stage of a corporate website. The real potential of virtual worlds lies in their convenience for demonstrating products in development to your coworkers, clients, and vendors; for working together on documents; and for creating flowcharts and managing project time lines. The tools that allow you to realize this potential are already available, even if they are not fully standardized at the present time. We do see strong development in this direction as both virtual world platform providers and third-party vendors rush to create a variety of collaboration tools that connect the Web and virtual worlds, import or export the output of 3-D modeling programs into virtual worlds, and allow the sharing of applications and media among virtual world users.

Corporate Training

Virtual worlds introduce an important new dimension to training—they let trainees learn by doing. As we noted in Chapter 2, virtual worlds take us into the world of experiential learning, instead of the "direct instruction" that is so prevalent in the training classrooms of today. Experiential learning allows us to acquire "tacit knowledge," which is embedded in our brains and bodies without us being conscious of it. This knowledge can be strengthened and generalized through conscious reflection of our experiences, so that both explicit and tacit knowledge are created in virtual world training experiences. This mix of virtual experiences reinforced by reflective exercises is especially appealing to younger employees, as they have come to expect a certain level of control and interactivity in most of their activities.

As in the case of collaborative work, this would be academic unless experiential training positively affected the bottom line—and it does. If faster and better learning are not compelling enough to convince you, how about avoiding costly mistakes? Experiential training works especially well for providing a safe environment where trainees can—and, in fact, are *expected* to—learn in part by making mistakes that would cause catastrophe in the real world.

Robert C. Amme, a research professor of physics at the University of Denver, contends that since "a new nuclear power plant hasn't been built in the United States for decades, there is a knowledge gap that could pose a serious problem if the country returns to the energy path it largely abandoned in the late 1970s but which may become more popular, given continuing concerns over the availability of oil from foreign sources and global warming." To help solve this problem, the University of Denver has built a nuclear reactor for student training in Second Life, "a place where there's no radiation, nuclear fallout or even laws of gravity" (Amme 2007 and 2009).

An example of a less spectacular but perhaps more common application is the use of Second Life by British Petroleum (BP) to train new gas station employees in the safety features of gasoline storage tanks and piping systems. BP built a 3-D model of a typical underground pipe system. "Trainees could 'see' underground and observe the effect of using safety devices to control the flow of gasoline. They were able to observe the workings of a very complex system in a way they could never have done in real life" (Galagan 2008).

Detailed case studies of enterprise architecture training at Michelin (Chapter 7) and nurse training at the University of Kansas Medical School (Chapter 10) demonstrate the expansion of virtual worlds into technical and procedural training and into corporate communications. These types of training will be significantly enhanced by the use of new tools that are just starting to appear: robotic avatars, remote controls that sense precise hand movements (such as the Wii remote), and more realistic 3-D environments and models.

Leadership Development and Teamwork

Do a Google search on terms such as "Leadership Development," "Change Management," or "Teamwork" and you will find plenty of companies that offer boot camps or wilderness trips to help employees strengthen team bonds, develop initiative, and practice leadership skills. Now, with virtual worlds, you do not need to force your team to march twenty miles across a swamp to achieve these objectives. Virtual worlds offer tools that allow you to model specific situations, record people's actions both on an individual and a team level, and discuss results with the team.

Simulations to help you judge teamwork, attitude, leadership skills, and ability to stay cool under pressure are available today. There is little doubt that their number and applicability to real-life business situations will grow as the demand for effective methods of training increases. The trend at work here is the same one we see in other types of training and in collaboration: replacement of physical world "on-site" training with computer-based simulations made using video and flash technologies, and then virtual world training that incorporates the best features of both physical and virtual worlds. Virtual world training imitates the immersiveness of physical "on-site" training while bringing all the benefits of computer technology: the ability to run a simulation an unlimited number of times, to change the environment and simulation flow, to keep a record of each attempt, and to join a geographically dispersed team in real time.

Predicting Change with Technology Innovation Life Cycles

All technologies have a relatively predictable growth pattern that starts with vision and innovation and ends up with commercialization and adoption (if the technology is successful). In thinking about virtual worlds and employee training, we can see that the following are likely: changes in usage patterns, a proliferation of different kinds of virtual worlds with interoperability among them, rapid advances in technologies to support and improve virtual worlds, changes in human behaviors as virtual worlds become commonplace, and new business models that are designed to take advantage of some of the unique features of virtual worlds. Let's look at how this all may happen.

Clayton Christensen (2004) and his colleagues believe that it is possible to predict industry changes using theories of innovation. Essentially, technological change starts with a set of problems that require a solution, or at least a more effective way of dealing with them that would bring great benefit. In an open society, one in which experimentation with new ideas is encouraged and valued, individuals and groups are often working quietly in the background trying to solve these problems. This leads to the invention of new technologies and processes, and often multiple solutions or formulations are found.

As we have already noted, the first reaction to a new technology is an attempt to use it in the context of an old process. Almost simultaneously, the introduction of new technologies leads to the discovery of new ways of doing things that can be quite disruptive to those currently in power or to companies presently doing very well with the old methods. This is "the innovator's dilemma," observed Christensen in 1997, who noted that companies that are dominant in one period are rarely the leaders in the next wave of technological development.

Along with technical changes come new applications, content, uses, processes, and services. Then, a full-blown industry around the new technology can blossom, and at later stages, companies can offer integrated *solutions* that bundle technologies, applications, and services together. As time passes, new problems arise. Inventors and entrepreneurs start tinkering and experimenting, and the cycle starts all over again.

This pattern can be seen in the growth of virtual worlds. As the technology starts to settle down into a "dominant design," new applications, uses, and services are being found for virtual worlds. One of the early uses for virtual worlds has been in developing new approaches to employee training. At the same time, business requirements are already necessitating changes and additional functionality of the virtual world platforms.

By looking at what's happening in university laboratories, corporate research and development departments, and experimental sites from various vendors, it is possible to piece together a view of coming changes in virtual world technologies. There are many new developments that can be anticipated over the next decade. They include:

▶ Improved hardware and network infrastructure
▶ Increased realism in avatars, 3-D objects, and 3-D environments
▶ Improved tools for creating customized virtual worlds
▶ Multiple virtual worlds and metaverses (universes of multiple interconnected virtual worlds) with interoperability
▶ New multimodal input devices
▶ Distributed sources of content and rendering
▶ Increased use of virtual agents
▶ Convergence of virtual worlds with other learning technologies
▶ Mixing of real life and virtual worlds through augmented reality technologies, including the use of 3-D video cameras

These changes in the physicality of virtual worlds will, in turn, lead to behavioral changes in the individuals and groups utilizing the new possibilities of virtual worlds. The behavioral changes will create new business opportunities for those companies that are able to track and exploit them.

Given the newness of virtual worlds, it is easy to predict that they will grow significantly over the next ten years. Heather Havernstein, in a report from Forrester Research, stated that "within five years [virtual worlds] will become as important as the Web is today" (Havernstein 2008). In 2007 Wagner James Au predicted that the virtual world population would grow to fifty million by 2011. Au admitted that this figure was likely conservative, given that predictions were for twenty-six million virtual world residents from China alone in 2011. Microsoft has argued that virtual worlds or immersive environments will emerge as one of the dominant user experience waves by 2010 to 2015 and will be the dominant user experience after 2014.

This growth in the population of virtual worlds will be driven by rapid increases in the power and scope of virtual world technologies and an expansion in the basic infrastructure of the Internet. Increased bandwidth and much faster computers will improve the user experience, attracting even more users into virtual spaces in a kind of "virtuous circle."

Innovations in Virtual World Technologies

We know from Moore's Law that the power of computer technologies is roughly doubling every twenty months. So far, Moore has been right, and the impact of his insight does not show any signs of letting up. For example, according to Tinari (2008), the new all-optical Internet that is presently being constructed will have ten thousand to one hundred thousand times the capacity of the first version of the Internet, introduced in the 1980s. He adds, "The result will be hyper-realistic avatars that will be able to interact with others in ways that will be indistinguishable from living beings. The ultimate experience will be a full sensual immersion so that the user will be unable to distinguish reality from digital reality."

The increased realism will apply not only to the 3-D environments that make up virtual worlds but also to avatars and objects in these worlds. The next step in the creation of realistic avatars is the development of software that will turn 2-D photographs into realistic 3-D models of avatars and other objects. Beyond that, the creation of body doubles will proliferate and will be used for more realistic avatars as well as therapeutic uses, such as allowing obese persons to see what their bodies might look like after weight loss. Motek Medical in Amsterdam has already developed a system that creates virtual body doubles using motion-capture software and a suit with forty-seven reflective markers in the positions of specific muscles.

Smith (2008) says that in new virtual worlds being developed for the U.S. Army, new physics-based objects, more accurate weather simulations, and terrain modeling will finally put the "reality" into virtual reality. Realism will also be enhanced by tighter network connections between applications to eliminate lag time and latency effects. All this will be happening at the same time to create multiple simulations in the army's virtual environment.

The issue of realism is a subtle one. Research with robots shows that achieving partial realism can be unsettling to humans, since a robot who is almost perfectly realistic but without emotion creates the sense of a human who is not quite "all there." As a result, in virtual worlds, intensive work is being done to increase the "emotional bandwidth" for avatars, including the development of realistic two-way voice interaction and enhanced "emotional expression." The expression of emotions can even be linked to the avatar's owner, who can be automatically monitored for facial expressions that indicate his or her emotions.

Part of the projection of emotions in virtual worlds will be through innovations in the field of *haptics*—technologies based on the sense of touch or force feedback. Already we see technologies that use haptics to convey emotions, such as a "hug shirt" and a "kiss phone." Virtual interpersonal touch within 3-D worlds is coming soon to your monitor or mobile device. This work is still in the development phase for the most part, but several prototypes are available that demonstrate the power of "surface computing." We see haptics as a way to not only convey emotions but provide tactile feedback when you perform tasks such as operating a car, a scalpel, or a piece of machinery in a virtual world simulation.

Another promising technology—the reproduction of realistic avatars from holographic projections of real people—seems almost to have come from the pages of science fiction. The state of this technology was demonstrated in November 2008 when CNN used holographic projections of remote reporters to convey their virtual presence in the CNN studio where they interacted with live commentators. With the coming of 3-D television, future 3-D virtual worlds may be projected out of all sorts of devices, including screens and wristwatches.

 ## Improved Tools for Creating Customized Virtual Worlds

One of the main trends in virtual world technology is interoperability and, by extension, the ability to use custom content you create across all, or at least many, virtual worlds. Virtual world platforms that can overcome their competitiveness in favor of a joint standard that allows avatars to travel from world to world, keeping the inventory of their objects, will attract users away from the closed platforms, changing the relative market share of different virtual worlds.

In a 2008 white paper, Sun Microsystems advocated for the building of "enterprise-grade" virtual world platforms with the following characteristics: scalability and distribution, reliability and security, flexibility for both public and private uses, and the availability of cutting-edge features and services (Sun Microsystems 2008).

The expansion of virtual worlds from a set of independent environments to an interconnected metaverse of many virtual worlds will be possible only with the development of common standards that allow interoperability among various 3-D platforms.

The Sun white paper suggests that this will happen through a number of needed innovations:

- ► Universal registered names and avatars to enable the transport of virtual identities and virtual assets between virtual worlds
- ► Common and portable identities such as Open ID (interoperable identities)
- ► Standards-based security for transactions involving digital assets
- ► Better-defined protocols and file formats such as X3D, the ISO standard for real-time 3-D computer graphics
- ► Universal clients, including standard 2-D and 3-D browsers on various types of devices (including mobile clients) with the ability to bookmark virtual worlds
- ► Integration with existing business applications

Interoperability standards for virtual worlds are now being worked on and negotiated. While some virtual worlds will remain separate proprietary domains for the near future, having open standards will greatly assist the development of future worlds. The signs of such a movement are there, from meetings to talk about standards to the development of bridging applications for instant messaging between OpenSim and Second Life.

Ultimately, virtual worlds as a technology will not belong to any single company but will be distributed across networks that allow for movement of avatars and the sharing of resources. This vision of "distributed simulations" has already been implemented by the U.S. Army, and "distributed virtual environments" based on "cloud computing" (a new term that refers to the fact that information on the Internet is sort of floating out there, accessible from anywhere) and peer-to-peer resource sharing are now in development.

This architecture, sometimes called "edge computing," allows for the distributed rendering of vast territories, allowing huge virtual worlds to be created in the near future. This is already happening on an experimental basis; for example, Chaudhuri et al. (2008) describe:

> . . . a system for distributed rendering of large and detailed virtual worlds. A cluster of servers create and maintain a hierarchical representation of the world that can be propagated to an unlimited number of clients through a content-distribution network. The pre-processing is easy to parallelize and storage requirements are minimal. Using a small subset of the representation, a client can explore a large and detailed world in real time on consumer hardware over a commodity Internet connection. The required bandwidth is independent of the size of the world. We report extensive performance measurements with a 2,500-square-kilometer world, densely populated with objects comprising 10 billion polygons.

These innovations are still in the early stages of development, but the vision and direction of the field of virtual world creation is clear.

 ## New Multimodal Input Devices

Most virtual worlds such as Second Life rely on input from a computer keyboard and mouse. This is about to change, as many more ways of influencing and controlling a virtual world environment become possible. Look for adaptations of gaming controllers to be used to control avatars and to build and operate objects in virtual worlds. The Wii Remote from Nintendo has already been used successfully for Second Life–based training of employees in a pest control company and in a major logistics company (Mollman 2007). Data input can come from many sources, including:

▶ Gaming controllers and consoles
▶ Digital cameras
▶ Motion capture software

- ▶ Voice input and voice recognition software
- ▶ Mobile phones
- ▶ Devices to read RFID and optical tags
- ▶ Geographical positioning system (GPS) devices
- ▶ Haptic devices
- ▶ Neural interfaces
- ▶ Data mining of large collections and data streams

Already, applications such as Microsoft's Photosynth can read thousands of photographs of a particular location from the Flickr.com website and stitch them together to build 3-D simulations of that building or place. The possible ways of navigating and controlling such an application could range from using your hands to indicate meaningful gestures to carrying out actions through an avatar in-world. Multi-touch sensing with large motor movements was demonstrated as a concept by a character played by Tom Cruise in the movie *Minority Report*, where he moved large objects using a multi-touch screen. Now this technology is available in reality through the work of Jeff Han at MIT (who was a consultant for the film).

Moreover, technology is being developed to allow "closely coupled collaboration" where the movements of users in different physical locations can be used to coordinate collaborative activities in a virtual world, such as dancing or other group activities. These innovations in virtual world navigation mean that nonprofessional visitors in a virtual environment should be able to find their way around without previous training and, when they need help, to initiate a conversation with a personal agent using natural language dialogue (Van Dijk et al. 2003).

As noted, virtual worlds are coming to the newest generation of mobile phones. As of June 2008, Second Life became available on mobile phones with 3G or WiFi capabilities through Vollee, an application that can be downloaded on at least seventy different mobile phones and can actually run the Second Life application. It makes it possible to send instant messages to someone in-world or for Second Life residents to send instant messages to enabled mobile phones. Another application from Comverse

Technology allows you to run Second Life on Java-enabled mobile phones and integrates text messaging with streaming video directly in-world. And Google has developed Android, an open source mobile phone platform that will be able to access multiple virtual worlds including Second Life.

Increased Use of Virtual Agents

Virtual worlds are inhabited by avatars standing in for human beings who control them, as well as by robotic avatars that are controlled by computer programs. The second type of avatar is also known as a "virtual agent." Both types of avatars coexist in virtual worlds and interact with each other.

One obvious use of virtual agents is to assist human-controlled avatars when they need help. Using natural dialogue or menus, virtual agents can assist with navigation or search functions, among other things. Of course, it is likely that some virtual agents will be created for malicious purposes, creating conflict and fear within a virtual world.

Scientists have been meeting for at least nine years to discuss these issues at the annual International Conference on Intelligent Virtual Agents. By looking at the titles of the papers presented over the past few years, we can get a good idea of where this field is headed. Themes that can be identified from proceedings of the most recent conference include:

- ► **Believability in virtual agents.** Here, work is being done on conversational behaviors such as gaze, gestures, and displays of emotion.
- ► **Cultural differences among virtual agents.** This includes work on the portrayal of cultural differences among agents, and issues of racism; i.e., do virtual humans elicit skin tone biases consistent with real-world skin tone biases.
- ► **Crowd simulation.** Crowds can be simulated by using groups of virtual agents.

▶ **Virtual therapy.** Virtual agents can serve as therapists.
▶ **Virtual institutions.** This includes work on creating normative environments that facilitate imitation learning in virtual agents based on regulations for a given virtual world.
▶ **The value of virtual beings.** Why do we need to have human characteristics at all in agents?

The strongest argument for virtual agents is that in simulations, we can use generic characters such as a "virtual standard patient," "virtual angry customer," "virtual difficult coworker," "virtual salesperson," "virtual receptionist," and any other actors that real people need to deal with in real life, with the word "virtual" simply signifying the location of training in a virtual world and the fact that there is no human being behind that agent—only a computer program. The result of all this research is that "a new paradigm for education and training is emerging: face-to-face interaction with intelligent animated agents (or embodied agents) in interactive learning environments. These pedagogical embodied agents must be capable of performing tasks and achieving goals individually and in collaboration with other agents, human and nonhuman" (Mahmood and Ferneley 2006).

 ## Integration and Convergence of Virtual Worlds with Other Learning Technologies

In the end, using virtual worlds for training, recruiting, and orientation will not happen in isolation from other efforts to improve the functioning of human resources management. Instead, we will see a convergence and "mashup" of many different technologies coming together in an integrated fashion to provide the best possible learning experience for employees. This, in turn, will lead to new ways of working and acting in organizational environments.

Integration

Implementing virtual world training does not mean that you will have to immediately abandon other training tools you worked hard to create. On the contrary, virtual world training complements them. As virtual worlds gain more acceptance as a valid platform for corporate training, there will be more and more emphasis on blending virtual world learning modules into the overall structure of the corporate e-learning program.

Simulations built in a business-oriented virtual world can be integrated with your learning management system (LMS). Doing so will immediately allow you to register learners for a VW class, create class requirements, allow the instructor to see the results of self-training through a familiar LMS interface, and incorporate virtual worlds in your training routine. Virtual world training becomes just another module in your program. In February 2009, Forterra, along with their partners IDSI and Rustici Software, announced integration of shareable content object reference model (SCORM) content into its OLIVE software. The SCORM standard makes Web-based training content portable. It can be easily repurposed for distance learning purposes. Organizations that spent significant effort and resources to make their training SCORM-compliant now see that their investment in SCORM content can be leveraged in virtual worlds for training and learning purposes. Similarly, SCORM-compliant training modules can be created in Second Life and other business-oriented VW platforms.

Convergence

In an insightful white paper, Susan Kish (2007) notes that virtual worlds will likely converge with many other technologies to produce a very different view of the future of 3-D environments. She is convinced that there is a developmental process whereby virtual worlds become "virtual browsers," allowing them to be used as a more natural way of navigating the

Internet than the present windows metaphor. Almost everyone will have an avatar, and virtual worlds will be either fanciful or imitative of the "real world." We can see this confluence of forces already with the mixture of technologies that are represented in the new 3-D Web, exemplified by Google Earth. The result will be a post-Web environment that takes the 2-D Internet and transforms it into a 360-degree 3-D experience.

Convergence with other technologies including online gaming, console games, toys, digital music, business applications, and training simulations will create an infrastructure for collective intelligence and action. The combination of these "mashups" with the physical world will produce a wide variety of "mixed reality" or "augmented reality" learning experiences.

Examples of these new learning environments are just starting to appear. At the Universitat Jaume I in Castelló, Spain, psychologists are curing insect phobias using virtual cockroaches. The Virtual Great Barrier Reef simulation takes learners underwater off Australia in a "dive vehicle." Similarly, the University of British Columbia's Human Communications Lab is able to simulate the physical and visual sensations of swimming across the Pacific Ocean. More examples of the use of 3-D augmented reality can be found in new applications for training police, firefighters, and military personnel.

 ## Changes in Human Responses and Abilities in Virtual Worlds

While many applications of virtual worlds are simulations of real-world procedures and processes, the virtual world experience also has the potential of being transformative and disruptive. This is uncharted territory, and therefore it is not surprising that virtual worlds have the potential for producing new human responses and emerging skills that have not been seen before.

Looking ahead, the Gartner research firm predicts that collaboration in virtual worlds will have a significant effect on worldwide travel and that virtual meetings will cost the airline industry 2.1 million seats per year by 2012 (Gartner Research 2009). Certainly, virtual collaboration among colleagues has the potential to be a "killer app" for virtual world technologies. The new cluster of "technology for collaboration" combines virtual worlds, cloud computing, storage on demand, and next-generation networks.

As we have seen from the case studies in this book, virtual environments are becoming the new corporate meeting spaces, labs for practicing skills together without being together in the same physical space, and tools for interactive training even when you cannot interact with another human being. In 2009 the University of California Irvine received a $3 million grant to study how research, planning, collaboration, and communication in organizations can take place in virtual worlds. Massively multiplayer online games (MMOGs) and virtual worlds such as World of Warcraft and Second Life are of specific interest to these researchers.

Researchers at Stanford University and the University of California Berkeley are studying how students and teachers can enter the same virtual world and learn together and are comparing its benefits to those of video learning. The Stanford University website for the laboratory involved describes this research:

First, immersive settings allow users to see in full three dimensions, greatly increasing detail, presence (i.e., learners feel psychologically as if they are in the digital learning environment, as opposed to the physical space) and social presence (i.e., they feel as if the digital reconstruction of the instructor is a real person). Second, as opposed to stationary video, immersive virtual settings allow users to control how they view the environment by allowing them to change aspects such as camera position and orientation, even allowing a disconnect between their own representation and their point of view in real-time. Third, video settings only allow users to watch the instructor; immersive virtual reality allows the user to interact with the instructor and the environment, as well as to perform novel functions such as sharing body space with the instructor during learning. (VHIL 2009)

In the first experiment in this research, where students learned tai chi movements, the results suggested that "people learned more in the immersive virtual reality system than in the 2-D video system."

Already, says Tinari (2008), "Second Life is changing how companies design products and interact with their customers, how professors train medical students, how people explore ideas, interact, and have fun. Now virtual worlds will soon allow people to 'see their future selves' and help them to understand the impact of their actions, personal choices and behaviors." For example, by watching people burn calories on a treadmill, people are encouraged to exercise; by seeing themselves as elderly, they are encouraged to save for retirement.

Because we can increasingly create avatars that closely resemble ourselves, we can start to use this technology for behavioral modeling. Then, we can change our virtual selves in ways that would be difficult or impossible in the real world. We can rehearse "what if" scenarios to see what happens when we make certain decisions.

In what is being called "the Proteus Effect," social scientists are studying how our avatars may be changing us in both virtual and real environments. Do we become attached to our avatar, and do things that happen to our avatar affect how we feel about ourselves and others? In particular, can learning new behaviors in virtual environments lead to social transformations in real life? The answer appears to be yes. Interacting in virtual worlds can change our sense of self and the projection of oneself to others. And interactions in virtual worlds can be totally unlike anything we have experienced in real life.

We are, in fact, building a new social infrastructure for collective intelligence. Virtual worlds can serve as the new "brain" of an organization or even a society. But the drawback is that 3-D virtual world technology currently offers somewhat unregulated environments without the means to enforce norms of behavior and interaction rules on their inhabitants (Bogdanvych 2007). In response, we are inventing new institutions within virtual worlds to regulate and normalize this new space.

Impact on Business

Virtual worlds have the potential to be the central organizing environment for a particular firm. This environment becomes a new "corporate brain," the activity center that holds the enterprise together. Robert Cohen (2008) says, "With this center for intelligence in place, corporations will restructure hierarchical systems to create new ways to manage business operations and make strategic decisions."

The industrial corporation is based on the efficiencies of standardized procedures, command and control, and a view of the enterprise as a "well-oiled machine," whereas the postindustrial corporation is characterized by horizontal and vertical connections between employees. As a construct it might seem more loose and messy, but it is also more creative and networked—a much better organizational structure for stimulating innovation and solving problems. It is also a much harder structure to manage by means of top-to-bottom orders, and its success is dependent on well-organized opportunities for self-training.

Because of this shift, control of corporations is likely to move from a hierarchical model with levels of decision-making power to a model where all employees are empowered to think about and solve problems collaboratively within a relatively flat and multi-branched organizational structure. This should make large corporations more agile and responsive to new trends in a world where change is constant and problems are increasingly complex.

Employees will no longer be trained but "self-fashioned," operating within small groups, with both strong ties (within a small group) and weak ties (between small groups) that maximize information interchange. Of course, there will be resistance and a backlash from employees threatened by such changes. Steve Prentice, vice president and distinguished analyst at Gartner, groups the issues that companies could be facing in this change into these five categories:

1. IT-related security risks
2. Identity authentication and access management
3. Confidentiality
4. Brand and reputation risk management
5. Productivity

The stakes are high. Chris Melissinos, chief gaming officer at Sun, comments, "Virtual worlds are critical to adoption of next generation services. This will be a multimillion dollar marketplace across the board" (Farber 2007).

 ## Implications for the Future of Training

Given all the expected developments described in this chapter, what are the implications for the future of employee training? We see an impact on training in at least four areas:

1. **More realistic experiential training.** The experience of training is going to become much more realistic. Already we have the ability to fool our senses in such a way as to confuse virtual reality with physical reality. This will lessen the need for expert instruction as the principal form of training methodology. Instead of listening and taking notes, learners will experience and explore the actual situations for which they are training. Learning is becoming a more intense but also more playful activity.

2. **Decrease in the costs of powerful training technologies.** High-tech simulators, such as those used in flight training, are massively expensive pieces of equipment. In a few short years, the cost of virtual reality technologies has rapidly decreased to the point where they are relatively inexpensive to acquire, and often free to the end user. By creating immersive environments on mobile and handheld devices, virtual worlds will be available in everyone's pocket. This will bring powerful computing, data analysis, decision-making, and learning tools to employees of companies of any size.

3. **Less overall training, more active learning by collaboratively solving problems.** There is a tendency for companies, when introducing virtual worlds to employees, to have training sessions on how to use and behave within these new learning spaces. If the 3-D environment is properly designed and is intuitively easy to use, once employees learn how to operate their avatars, more training is not generally needed for them to benefit from their experiences in the virtual world. For complex situations it is beneficial to design automated helpers—such as directory signs—that will help new trainees navigate virtual worlds by simply transferring them to a correct location. In virtual worlds, the role of the instructor changes from a class "czar" to that of a "feedback provider" and "explainer of last resort." Employees can immerse themselves in real problems and work collaboratively with others to solve them largely without an instructor's help. This behavior can continue as employees make business decisions in real time and see the results immediately, leading to extremely agile businesses. It has been suggested that this method of learning from others in real time might lead to a modern "guild system" with levels of apprenticeship in the virtual world. This already happens in online games, such as World of Warcraft.

4. **The rise of collective intelligence and group learning.** The myth of individual genius has been debunked in Malcolm Gladwell's 2008 book, *Outliers*. In the book he shows how high achievement is the

result of not only individual abilities but also social support systems and good fortune. While rugged individualism has been an idealized value in American culture, it is a disadvantage when problems become too large for *any* individual to solve, regardless of ability. This "ingenuity gap" is one of the forces driving us into virtual worlds in order to work together more effectively. In the world of work, expertise now resides in the value chain, not in an individual self-contained corporation or in any one individual employee. Group learning makes a lot of sense, and we are definitively moving from individual to group learning—with an emphasis on team development, collaborative knowledge building, and collective intelligence. Working within virtual worlds facilitates these processes.

The work on virtual worlds and employee training being done today is the leading edge of a major transformation of how we learn as adults. It is time to get to work creating this new world, so full of opportunity and excitement!

References

Aldrich, C. 2003. *Learning by doing: A comprehensive guide to simulations, computer games, and pedagogy in e-learning and other educational experiences.* San Francisco: Pfeiffer—John Wiley & Sons.

Amme, R. 2007. In Second Life, there's no fallout. Inside Higher Education, Aug. 20. www.insidehighered.com/news/2007/08/20/secondlife.

Amme, R. 2009. Use of Second Life for interactive instruction and distance learning in nuclear physics and technology. Paper presented at the American Physics Association meetings, Denver, CO, May 2–5.

Au, W. J. 2007. Virtual world population: 50 million by 2011. Gigaom, May 20. http://gigaom.com/2007/05/20/virtual-world-population-50-million-by-2011.

Best, J. 2007. How Second Life changes customer service. BusinessWeek .com, April 10. www.businessweek.com/globalbiz/content/apr2007/gb20070410_481047_page_2.htm.

Boeing. 1995. Commercial airplanes. www.boeing.com/commercial/safety/airline_role.html.

Bogdanvych, A. 2007. Virtual institutions. Doctoral dissertation, University of Technology, Sydney, Australia.

Booz Allen Hamilton. 2006. The growth of global innovation networks creates new management challenges. www.boozallen.com/capabilities/services/services_article/3220998.

Borgmann, A. 1999. *Holding on to reality: The nature of information at the turn of the millennium.* Chicago: University of Chicago Press.

Brodkin, J. 2008. IBM, Second Life create business-friendly virtual worlds. NetworkWorld, April 3. www.networkworld.com/news/2008/040308-ibm-second-life-virtual.html.

BusinessWeek. 2006. It's not all fun and games. BusinessWeek.com, May 1. www.businessweek.com/magazine/content/06_18/b3982007.htm.

Chaudhuri, S., D. Horn, P. Hanrahan, and V. Koltun. 2008. Distributed rendering of virtual worlds. http://hci.stanford.edu/cstr/reports/2008-02.pdf.

Christensen, C. 1997. *The innovator's dilemma: When new technologies cause great firms to fail.* Boston: Harvard Business School Press.

Christensen, C., S. Anthony, and E. Roth. 2004. *Seeing what's next.* Boston: Harvard Business School Press.

Cohen, R. 2008. Virtual worlds and the transformation of business: Impacts on the U.S. economy, jobs, and industrial competitiveness. Working paper 04, Athena Alliance.

Costa, D. 2003. Second Life review. PC Magazine. www.pcmag.com/article2/0,4149,1306196,00.asp.

Crookall, D., R. L. Oxford, and D. Saunders. 1987. Towards a reconceptualization of simulation: From representation to reality. *Simulation/Games for Learning*, 17:147–71.

Cross, J., T. O'Driscoll, and E. Trondsen. 2006. Another life: Virtual worlds as tools for learning. eLearn Magazine. www.elearnmag.org/subpage.cfm?section=articles&article=44-1.

Davenport, T. H. 2005. *Thinking for a living: How to get better performances and results from knowledge workers.* Boston: Harvard Business School Press.

Dede, C. 1995. The evolution of constructivist learning environments: Immersion in distributed, virtual worlds. *Educational Technology*, 35(5): 46–52.

DeRosa, D., D. Hantula, N. Kock, and J. D'Arcy. 2004. Trust and leadership virtual teamwork: A media naturalness perspective. *Human Resource Management*, 43 (2/3): 219–32.

Dewey, J. 1938. *Experience and education.* New York: Collier Books.

Driver, E. 2008. Accenture recruiting in Second Life cost-effectively targets the "Facebook audience." ThinkBalm, Aug. 14. http://tiny url.com/67oes7.

Driver, E., P. Jackson, C. Moore, C. Shooley, and J. Barnett. 2008. Getting real work done in virtual worlds. Forrester Research, Inc.

Duarte, D., and N. Snyder. 2007. *Mastering virtual teams: Strategies, tools, and techniques that succeed.* 3rd ed. San Francisco: Jossey-Bass.

Ducheneaut, N., N. Yee, E. Nickell, and R. Moore. 2007. The life and death of online gaming communities: A look at guilds in World of Warcraft. Proceedings of the CHI 2007 Conference, San Jose, CA, April 28–May 3. http://tinyurl.com/344sap.

Edery, D., and E. Mollick. 2009. *Changing the game: How video games are transforming the future of business.* Upper Saddle River, NJ: FT Press.

Farber, D. 2007. The future of virtual worlds. Between the Lines Blog, Aug. 1. http://blogs.zdnet.com/BTL/?p=5825.

Forterra Systems. 2008. Forterra Customers. www.forterrainc.com/index.php/customers.

Fresh, E., J. Henderson, P. Fishwick, F. Futterknecht, and B. Hamilton. 2008. Second Life: Integrating traditional Web content with 3D cultural immersion. http://cero11.cise.ufl.edu/~webmaster/Down loadablecontent/Fresh-etal_SHUFE2008.pdf.

Fullan, M. 2001. *Leading in a culture of change.* San Francisco: Jossey-Bass.

Galagan, P. 2008. Second that, *T+D*, February, 34–37. www.astd.org/NR/rdonlyres/F3C38970-2C51-4437-9A4E-BDBA9703F2B0/15724/080234.pdf.

Garcia-Ruiz, M., A. Edwards, S. El-Seoud, and R. Aquino-Santos. 2008. Collaborating and learning a second language in a wireless virtual reality environment. *International Journal of Mobile Learning and Organisation*, 2(4): 369–77.

Gartner Research. 2009. Gartner predicts video telepresence will replace 2.1 million airline seats per year by 2012, losing the travel industry $3.5 billion annually. Press release, Sydney, Australia, February 6. www.gartner.com/it/page.jsp?id=876512.

Gee, J. P. 2006. Are video games good for learning? Keynote address to the Curriculum Corporation 13th National Conference, Adelaide, Australia. http://cmslive.curriculum.edu.au/verve/_resources/Gee_Paper.pdf.

Gladwell, M. 2008. *Outliers: The story of success*. New York: Little, Brown and Company.

Glass, W. 2005. Twelve ways to create a fun simulation. Forio's Forum. http://forio.com/resources/fun.

Gould, D. 2006. Virtual teams. Online paper. Fifth generation work—virtual organization. www.seanet.com/~daveg/vrteams.htm.

Graham, P. 2005. Web 2.0. www.paulgraham.com/web20.html.

Griffy-Brown, C., and M. Hamlin. 2003. Experiential e-learning as a mechanism for creating competency in information and security systems. Proceedings of the IACIS 2003 Conference, Las Vegas. www.iacis.org/iis/2003_iis/PDFfiles/Griffy-BrownHamlin.pdf.

Havernstein, H. 2008. Virtual worlds will soon be as important as web companies. Computerworld, January 9. www.computerworld.com/s/article/9056602/Virtual_worlds_will_soon_be_as_important_as_Web_to_companies.

Heinrichs, W. L., P. Youngblood, P. Harter, and P. Dev. 2008. Simulation for team training and assessment: Case studies of online training with virtual worlds. *World Journal of Surgery*, 32(2): 161–70.

Heiphetz, A., and S. Liberman. 2007. Training simulations and metrics in Second Life. Materials of Innovations in Learning Conference, San Jose, California.

Herrington, J., T. C. Reeves, and R. Oliver. 2007. Immersive learning technologies: Realism and online authentic learning, *Journal of Computing in Higher Education*, 19(1): 65–84.

Horwitz, F., D. Bravington, and U. Silvis. 2006. The promise of virtual teams: Identifying key factors in effectiveness and failure. *Journal of European Industrial Training*, 30(6): 472–94.

Huffhines, Aldon. 2008. World Bank's Second Life launch of "Doing Business" report. http://slnn.com/article/world-bank-doing -business-2009.

IBM. 2008. IBM and Linden Lab to explore enterprise-class solution for virtual world creation and collaboration. Press release. www-03.ibm .com/press/us/en/pressrelease/23800.wss.

IBM and Seriosity, Inc. 2007. Virtual worlds, real leaders. A Global Inno- vation Outlook 2.0 Report. www.ibm.com/ibm/gio/media/pdf/ibm _gio_gaming_report.pdf.

Jones, K. 1985. *Designing your own simulations.* New York: Methuen.

Kahai, S., E. Carroll, and R. Jestice. 2007. Team collaboration in virtual worlds. *DATA BASE for Advances in Information Systems*, 38(4): 61–68.

Kieran, C. 2007. Second Life and Google Earth are transforming the idea of architectural collaboration. Architectural Record (Tech Briefs). http://archrecord.construction.com/features/digital/archives/ 0701dignews-1.asp.

Kimball, L. 1997. Managing virtual teams. Presentation at the Team Strategies Conference, Toronto, Canada.

Kirkman, B., and J. Mathieu. 2004. The role of virtuality in work team effectiveness. Paper presented at the Academy of Management annual meeting, Louisiana, August 6–11.

Kirschner, P., J. Sweller, and R. Clark. 2006. Why minimal guidance during instruction does not work: An analysis of the failure of con- structivist, discovery, problem-based, experiential, and inquiry-based teaching. *Educational Psychologist*, 41(2): 75–86.

Kish, S. 2007. Virtual worlds: Second Life and the enterprise. Susan Kish Blog, August. http://skish.typepad.com/susan_kish/secondlife/SKish _VW-SL_sept07.pdf.

Kogler Hill, S. 2007. Team leadership. In Peter Northouse, ed., *Leadership: Theory and practice*. Thousand Oaks, CA: Sage, 207–35.

Kolb, D. 1984. *Experiential learning: Experience as the source of learning and development.* Englewood Cliffs, NJ: Prentice-Hall.

Lacan, J. 1977. *Ecrits: A selection.* Trans. A. Sheridan. New York: W. W. Norton and Company.

Leung, W. 2007. Recruiting real talent in a virtual world. Globe and Mail, July 16. www.theglobeandmail.com/servlet/story/RTGAM .20070716.wlrecruits16/BNStory/lifeMain.

Lewin, K. 1936. *Principles of topological psychology.* New York: McGraw-Hill.

Lively. 2008. Lively is closed. www.lively.com/goodbye.html.

Lloyd, S. 2006. *Programming the universe: A quantum computer scientist takes on the cosmos.* New York: Random House.

Luckner, J., and R. Nadler. 1997. *Processing the experience: Strategies to enhance and generalize learning.* Dubuque, IA: Kendall/Hunt.

Mahmood, A., and E. Ferneley. 2006. Embodied agents in e-learning environments: An exploratory case study. *Journal of Interactive Learning Research*, 17(2): 143–62.

Malhotra, A., and A. Majchrzak. 2005. Virtual workspace technologies. *MIT Sloan Management Review*, 46(2).

Manninen, T. 2002. Contextual virtual interaction as part of ubiquitous game design and development. *Personal and Ubiquitous Computing*, 6: 390–406.

Mark, R. 2007. Politics and Second Life: Virtual lobbying. Datamation, January 15. http://itmanagement.earthweb.com/article.php/3653976.

Massey, A. P., and M. Montoya. 2008. Managing the services lifecycle. *EDUCAUSE Review*, 43(5). www.educause.edu/EDUCAUSE+Review/ EDUCAUSEReviewMagazineVolume43/ManagingtheServicesLife cycle/163182.

Massey, A. P., M. Montoya, and V. Bartelt. 2009. Personal communication.

McLuhan, M., and Q. Fiore. 1967. *Medium is the massage: An inventory of effects.* New York: Bantam.

Mihhailova, G. 2007. Virtual teams: Just a theoretical concept or a widely used practice? *The Business Review*, 7(1): 186–92.

Mollman, S. 2007. Wii + Second Life = new training simulator. Wired. www.wired.com/gadgets/miscellaneous/news/2007/07/wiimote.

Montoya, M., and A. Massey. 2008. Presentation at roundtable "Starting corporate training program in Second Life: Best practices, security concerns, and future developments," in Second Life.

Moore, G. 1965. Cramming more components onto integrated circuits. *Electronics*, 38(8): 114–17.

Murphy, H. A., H. W. Hildebrandt, and J. P. Thomas. 1997. *Effective business communications*. New York: McGraw-Hill/Irwin.

Naone, E. 2007. Unreal meetings: Second Life's virtual conference rooms might be more useful if they didn't resemble their real-world counterparts. Technology Review, July 11. www.technologyreview.com/Infotech/19035/?a=f.

Nebolsky, C., N. Yee, V. Petrushin, and A. Gershman. 2003. Corporate training in virtual worlds. www.iiisci.org/journal/CV$/sci/pdfs/P674 230.pdf.

Norris, J. 2009. Healthcare support groups in online virtual worlds. http://john-norris.net/extras/VirtualWorlds/VirtWorldSupport Intro.pdf.

Northouse, P. 2007. *Leadership: Theory and practice.* Thousand Oaks, CA: Sage.

O'Connell, T. A., J. Grantham, K. Workman, and W. Wong. 2009. Leveraging game-playing skills, expectations, and behaviors of digital natives to improve visual analytic tools. *Journal of Virtual Research*, 2(1): 3–24.

O'Driscoll, T. 2007. Learning in three dimensions: Experiencing the sensibilities and imagining the possibilities. Video, posted to YouTube .com. www.youtube.com/watch?v=O2jY4UkPbAc.

Platt, M. 2009. Microsoft architecture overview. http://msdn.microsoft .com/en-us/library/ms978007.aspx.

Pogorzelski, S., and J. Harriott. 2007. *Finding keepers: The monster guide to hiring and holding the world's best employees.* New York: McGraw-Hill.

Polanyi, M. 1966. *The tacit dimension.* London: Routledge & Kegan Paul.

Polanyi, M. 1974. *Personal knowledge: Towards a post-critical philosophy.* Chicago: University of Chicago Press.

Powell, A., G. Piccoli, and B. Ives. 2004. Virtual teams: A review of current literature and directions for future research. *Database for Advances in Information Systems*, 35(1): 6–36.

Prensky, M., ed. 2001. *Digital game-based learning.* New York: McGraw-Hill.

Quinn, C. 2008. Virtual worldly. Learnlets, the Quinnovation Blog, June 1. http://blog.learnlets.com/?p=335.

Reuters. 2007. Forterra announces developer programs to enable customers and partners to create and deploy. Press release. www.reuters.com/article/pressRelease/idUS132291+05-Dec-2007+BW20071205.

Rickel, J., and W. L. Johnson. 1999. Virtual humans for team training in virtual reality. Proceedings of the Ninth International Conference on AI in Education, July, 578–85. www.isi.edu/isd/VET/vet.html.

Rogers, C. 1969. *Freedom to learn: A view of what education might become.* Columbus, OH: Charles E. Merrill.

Ryle, G. 1949. *The concept of mind.* Chicago: University of Chicago Press.

Schön, D. 1995. *The reflective practitioner: How professionals think in action.* New York: Basic Books.

Schrage, M. 1995. *No more teams: Mastering the dynamics of creative collaboration.* New York: Currency Doubleday.

Scola, N. 2007. Avatar politics: The social applications of Second Life. www.ipdi.org/UploadedFiles/Avatar%20Politics.pdf.

Second Life Blog. 2008. IBM and Linden Lab interoperability announcement. http://blog.secondlife.com/2008/07/08/ibm-linden-lab-interoperability-announcement.

Sherman, G., and R. Tillies. 2007. Educational research and evaluation data collection procedures in Second Life. In T. Bastiaens and S. Carliner, eds., Proceedings of World Conference on E-Learning in Corporate, Government, Healthcare, and Higher Education, 7365–73.

Smith, P. 1986. Instructional simulation: Research, theory, and a case study. Paper presented at the Annual Convention of the Association for Educational Communications and Technology, Las Vegas, NV (ERIC Document Reproduction Service No. ED 267 793).

Smith, R. 2008. Simulation in the 21st century. Presentation to Modsim World Conference 2008, Virginia Beach, VA. www.slideshare.net/ roger.smith/simulation-in-the-21st-century-presentation.

Social Science Research Institute, Pennsylvania State University. 2008. Virtual world offers new locale for problem solving. www.ssri.psu .edu/news/092908.htm.

Sun Microsystems. 2008. Current reality and future vision: Open virtual worlds. White paper. www.sun.com/service/applicationserversub scriptions/OpenVirtualWorld.pdf.

TechRadar. 2008. Second Life beats real life for collaboration. www.tech radar.com/news/internet/second-life-beats-real-life-for-collaboration -471985.

Teleplace. 2009. Customers. www.teleplace.com/company/customers.php.

Tinari, P. 2008. The future of virtual worlds. Online presentation, Pacific Institute for Advanced Study. www.wfs.org/2008presentations/tin ari.pdf.

Townsend-Gard, E., and E. Arnold. 2008. Second Life: Research, communication, and organization in a virtual world. www.aplici.org/con ferences/2008/Townsend-Gard_presentation.pdf.

Trotta, H., and D. Mirliss. 2007. Team building in virtual worlds. Presentation at the Mid-Atlantic Regional Conference. http://net.educause .edu/ir/library/pdf/MAC07067A.pdf.

Turing, A. 1950. Computing machinery and intelligence. *Mind*, 59:433–60.

Van den Hooff, B. 2009. Decision making in virtual worlds: An experiment. Future Workspaces, February 2. www.futureworkspaces.nl/ 2009/02/02/decision-making-in-virtual-worlds-an-experiment.

Van Dijk, B., R. op den Akker, A. Nijholt, and J. Zwiers. 2003. Navigation assistance in virtual worlds. *Informing Science Journal*, 6:115–25.

Virtual Human Interaction Lab (VHIL). 2009. Learning in immersive VR. http://vhil.stanford.edu/projects.

Virtual Social Worlds and Libraries blog. 2007. Activeworlds not Second Life? The choice is in the budget. http://vbiworld.blogspot.com/2007/11/activeworlds-not-second-life-choice-is.html.

Woodill, G. 2008. *Computer supported collaborative learning for training and development: Research and practice.* Sunnyvale, CA: Brandon Hall Research.

Index